This Kitten Coloring Book Belongs To:

_____

Copyright 2020 ColorMeMerry.com

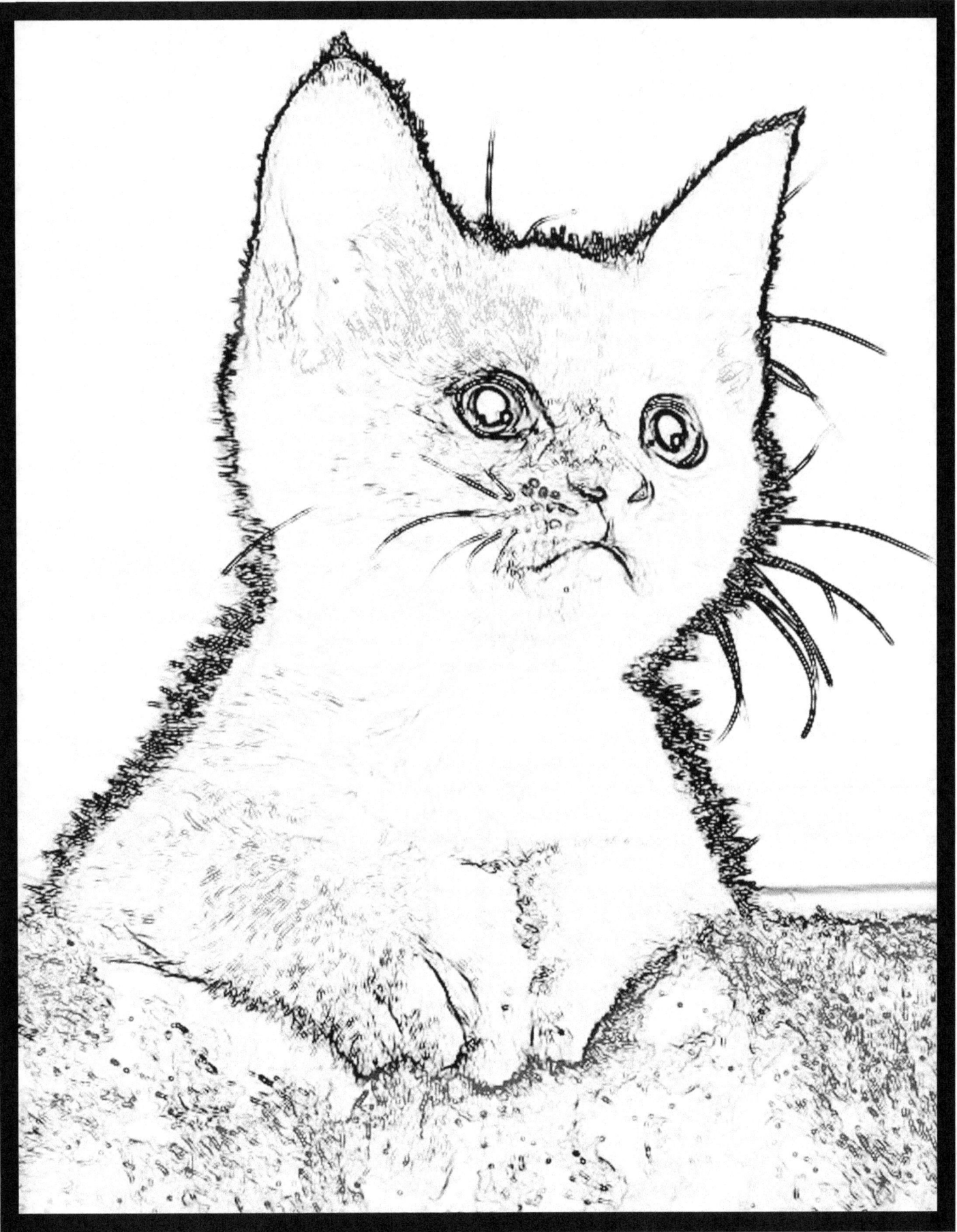

What do kitties like to eat on a hot day?

A Mice Cream Cone!

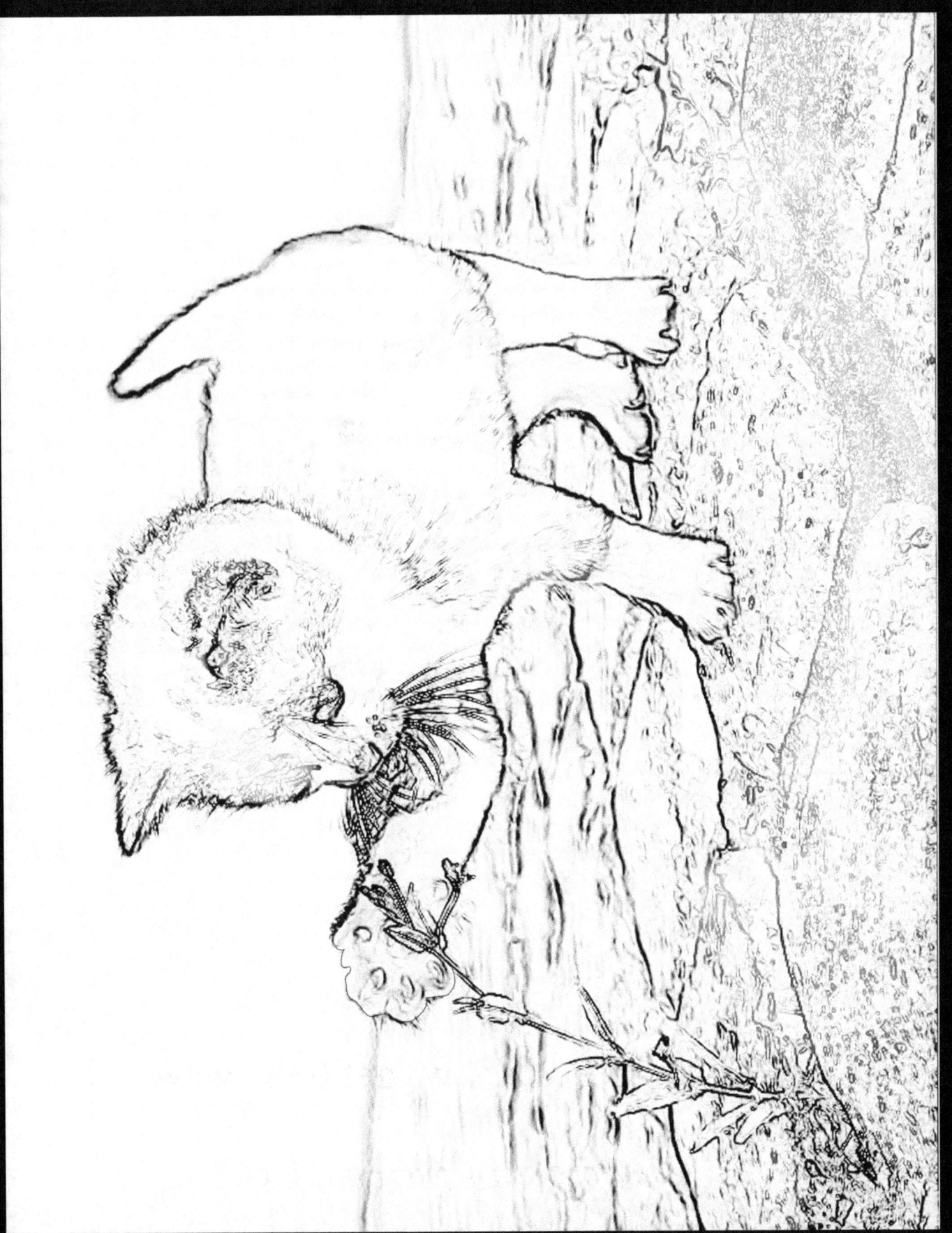

Why do kitties always get their way?

They are very purr-suasive!

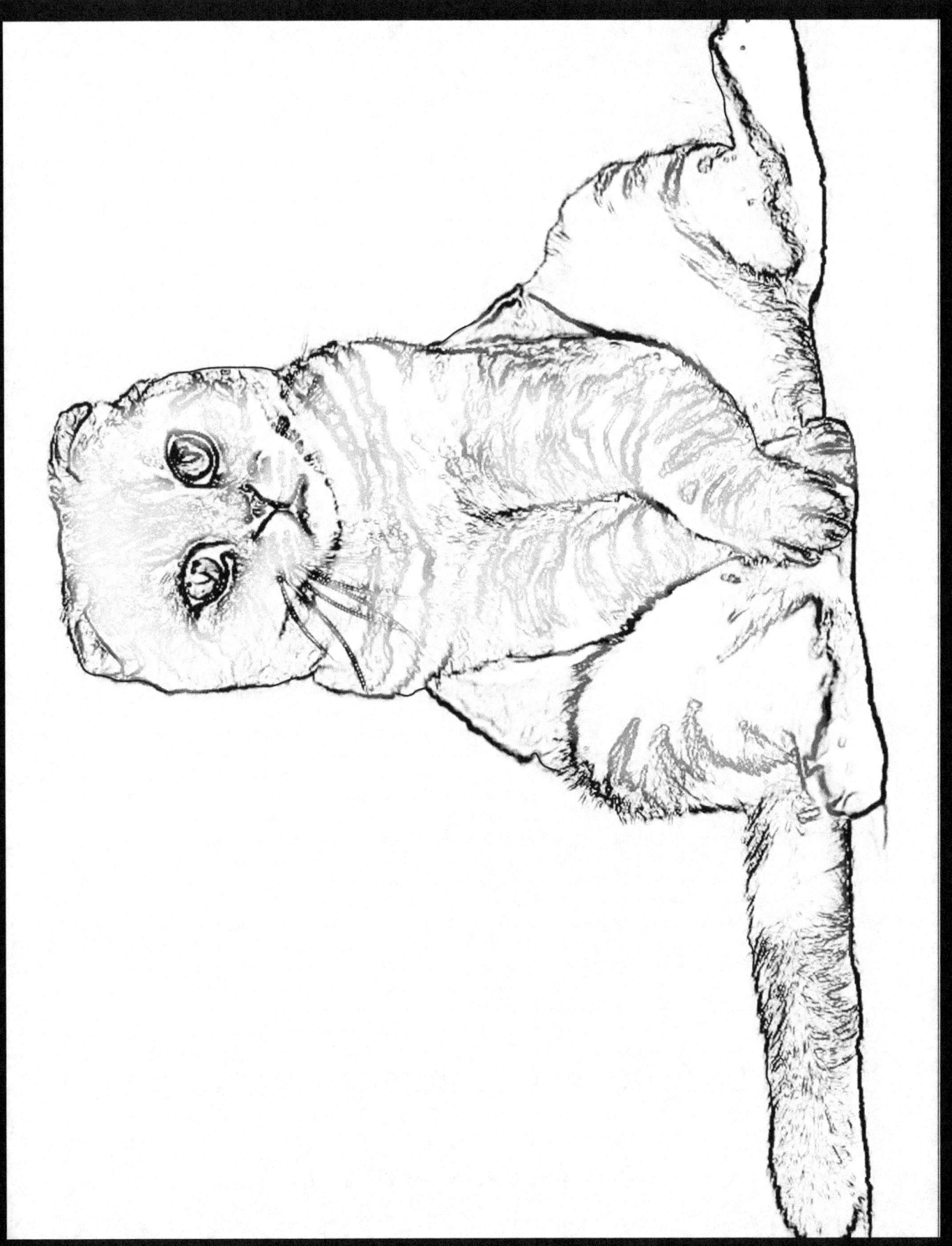

How do two kitties end a fight?

They hiss and make up!

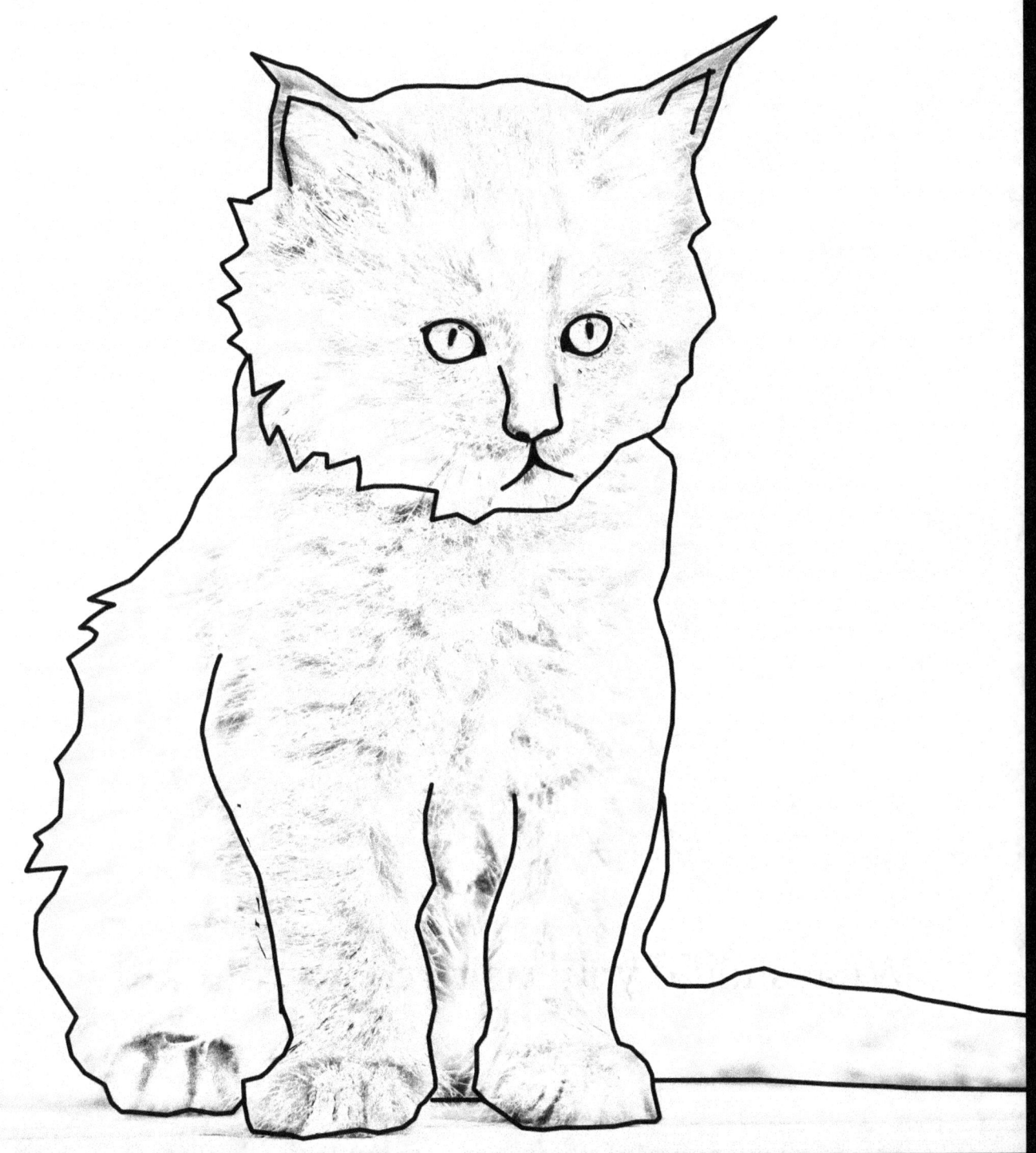

What should you use to comb your kitty?

A Catacomb!

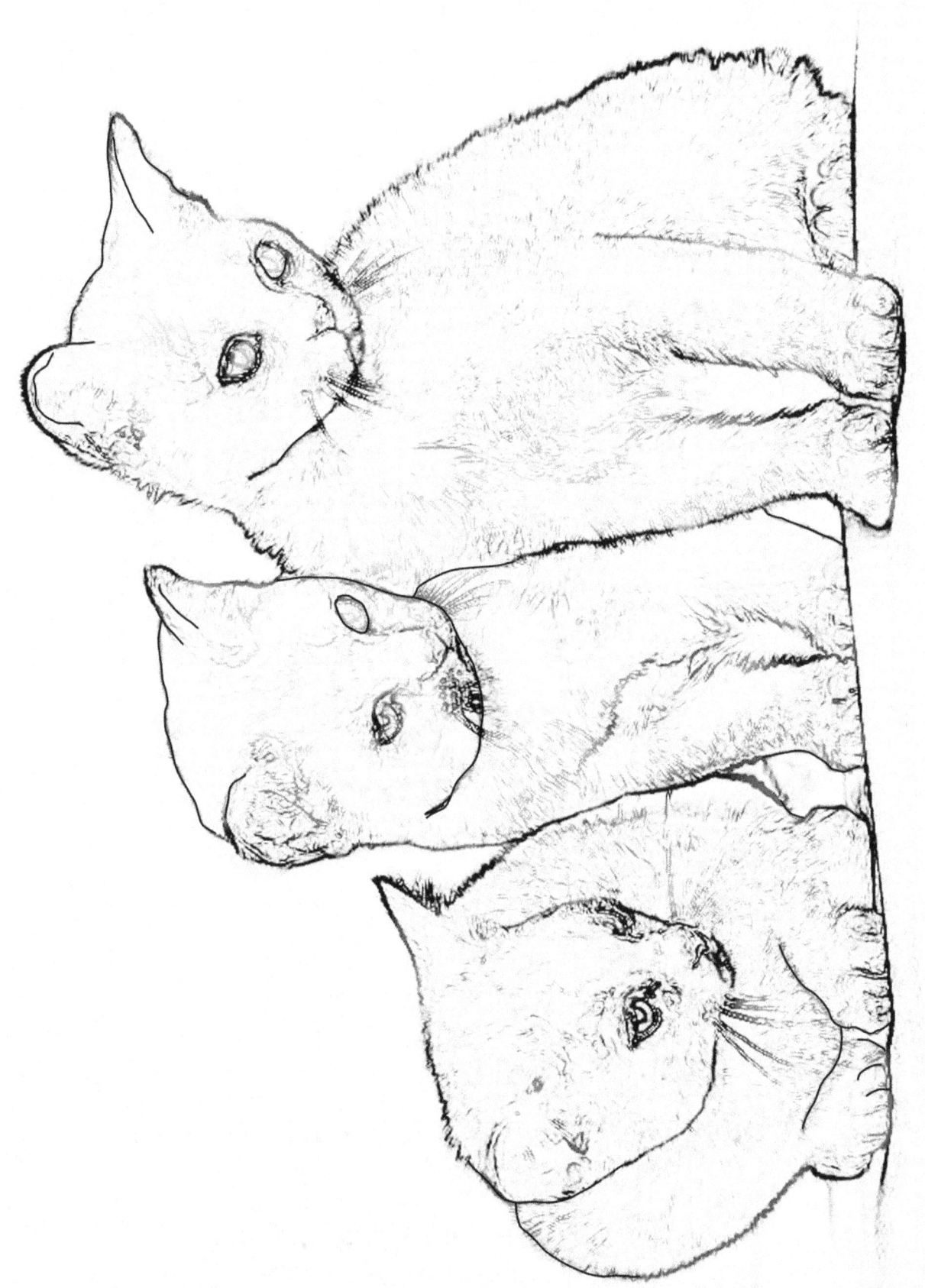

What is your kitty's favorite movie?

The Sound of Mewsic!

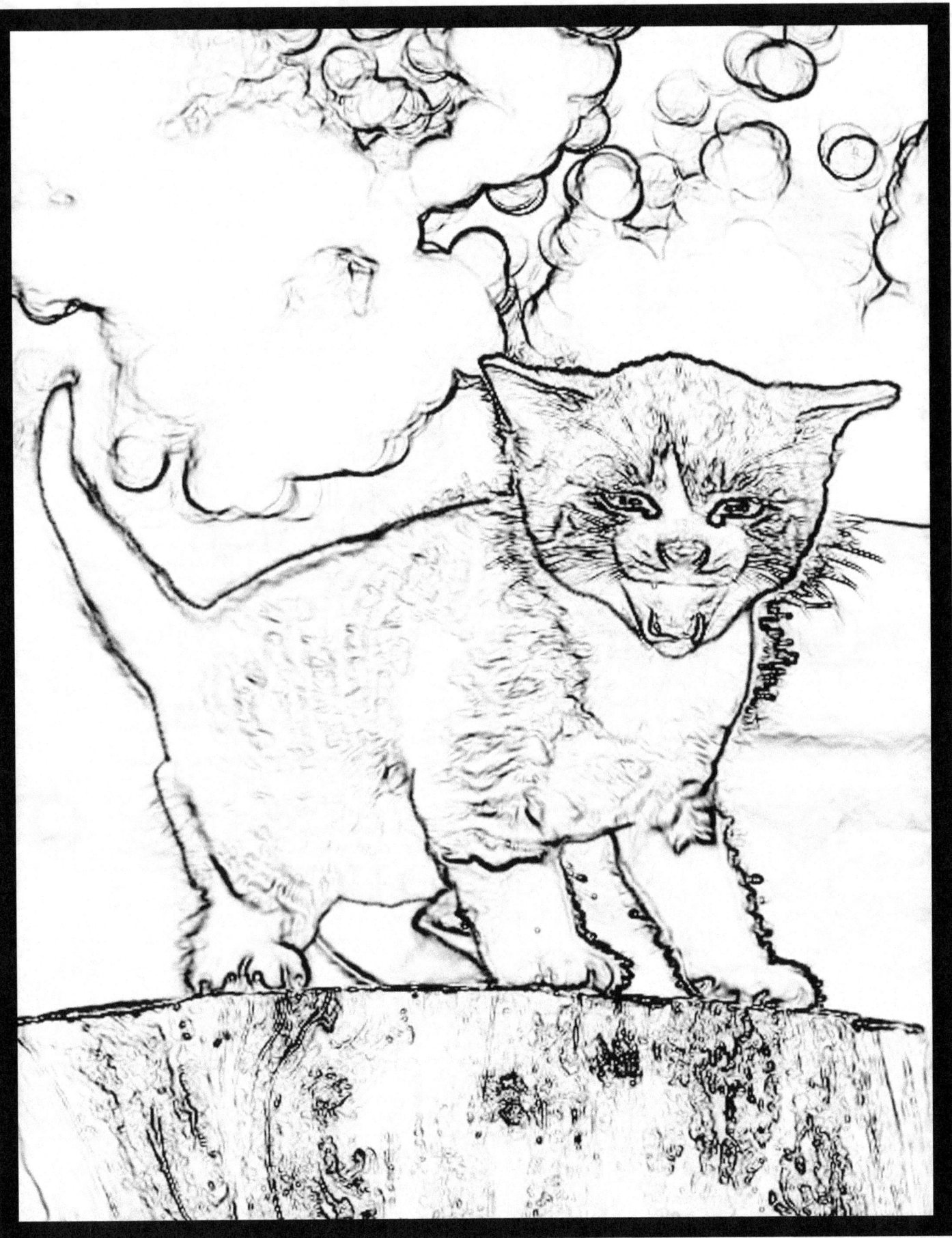

How do you know when your kitty is agitated?

She's having a hissy fit!

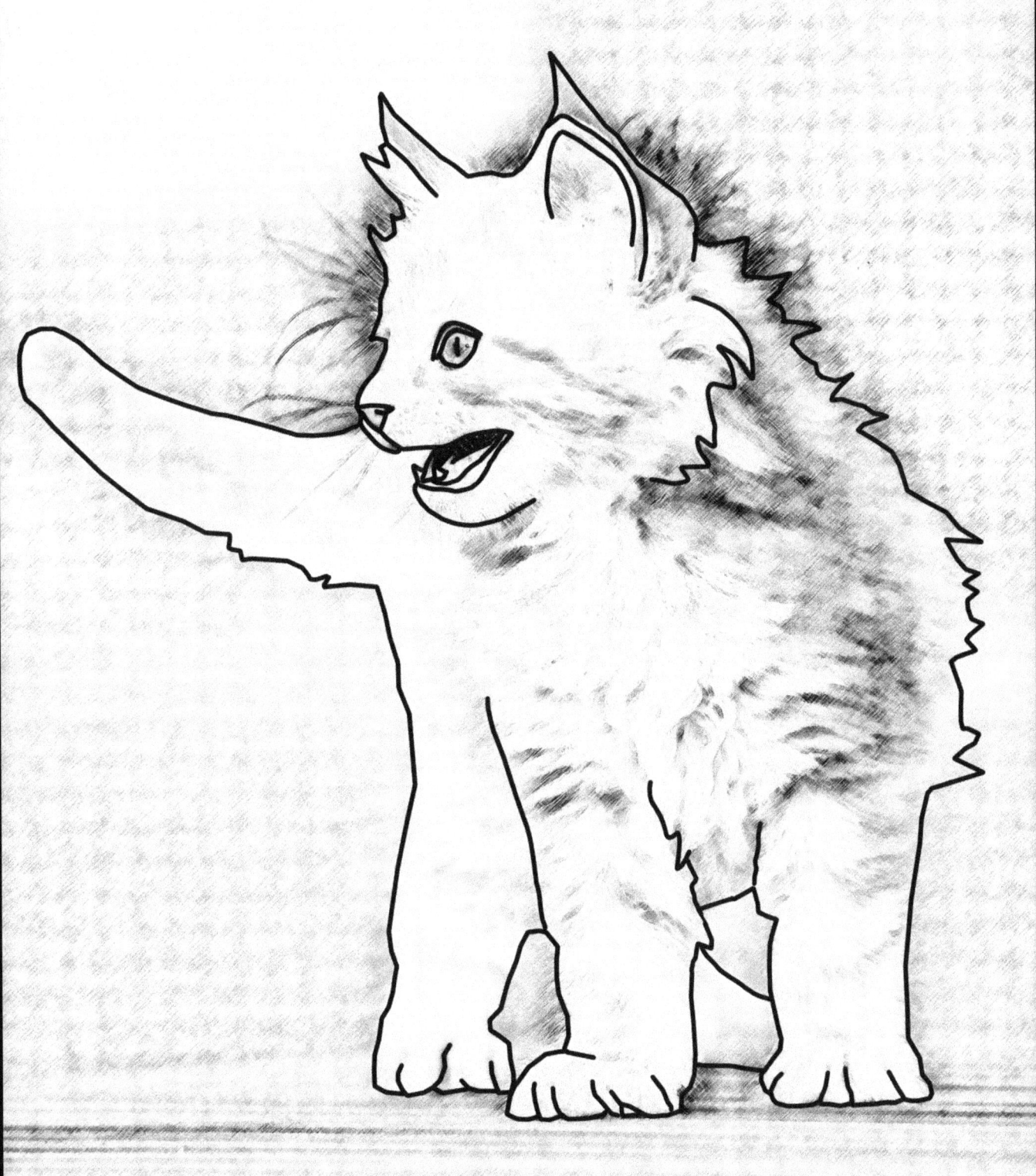

What's your kitty's favorite magazine?

Good Mousekeeping!

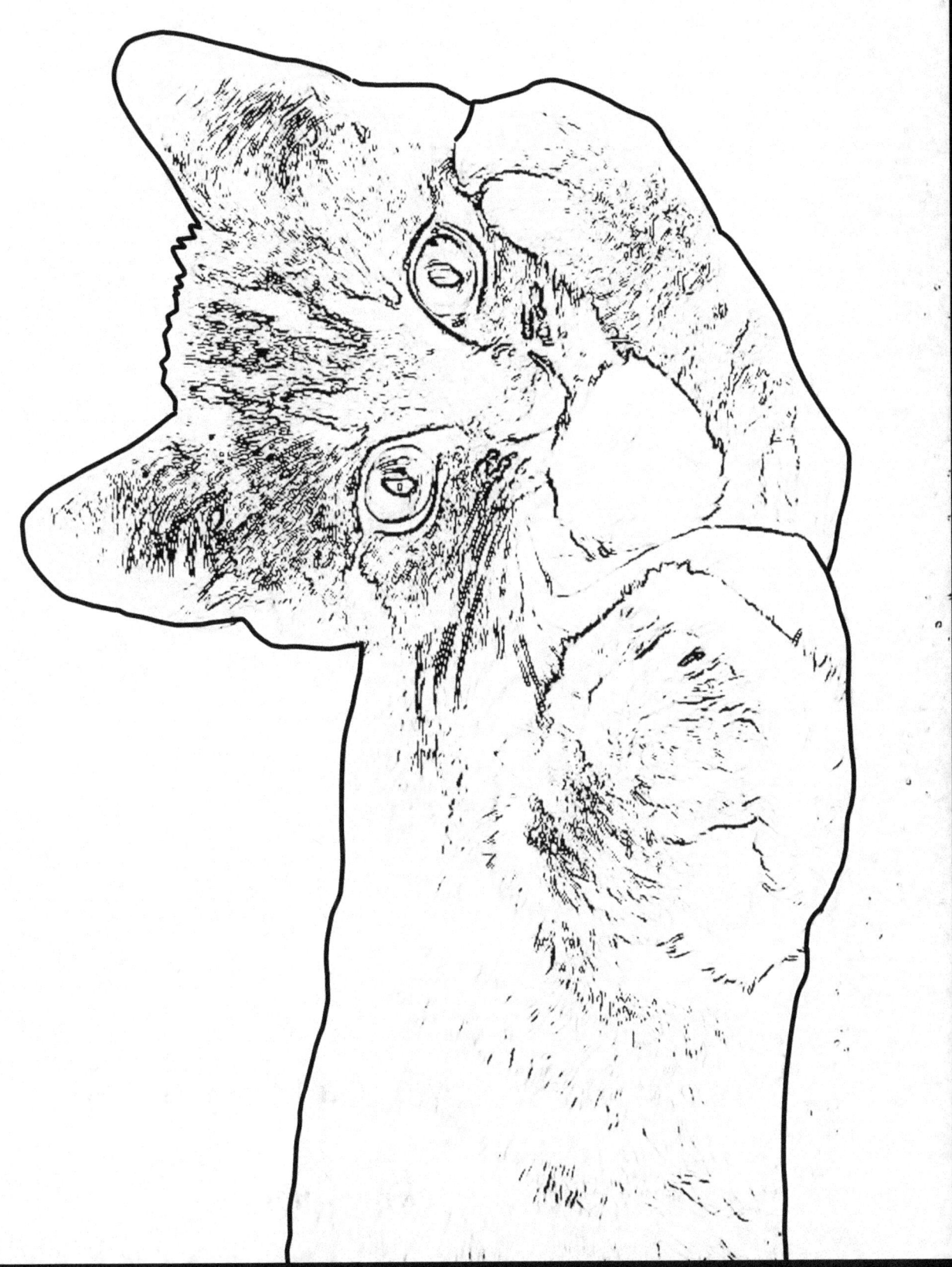

Why did the kitty wear a fancy dress?

She was feline fine!

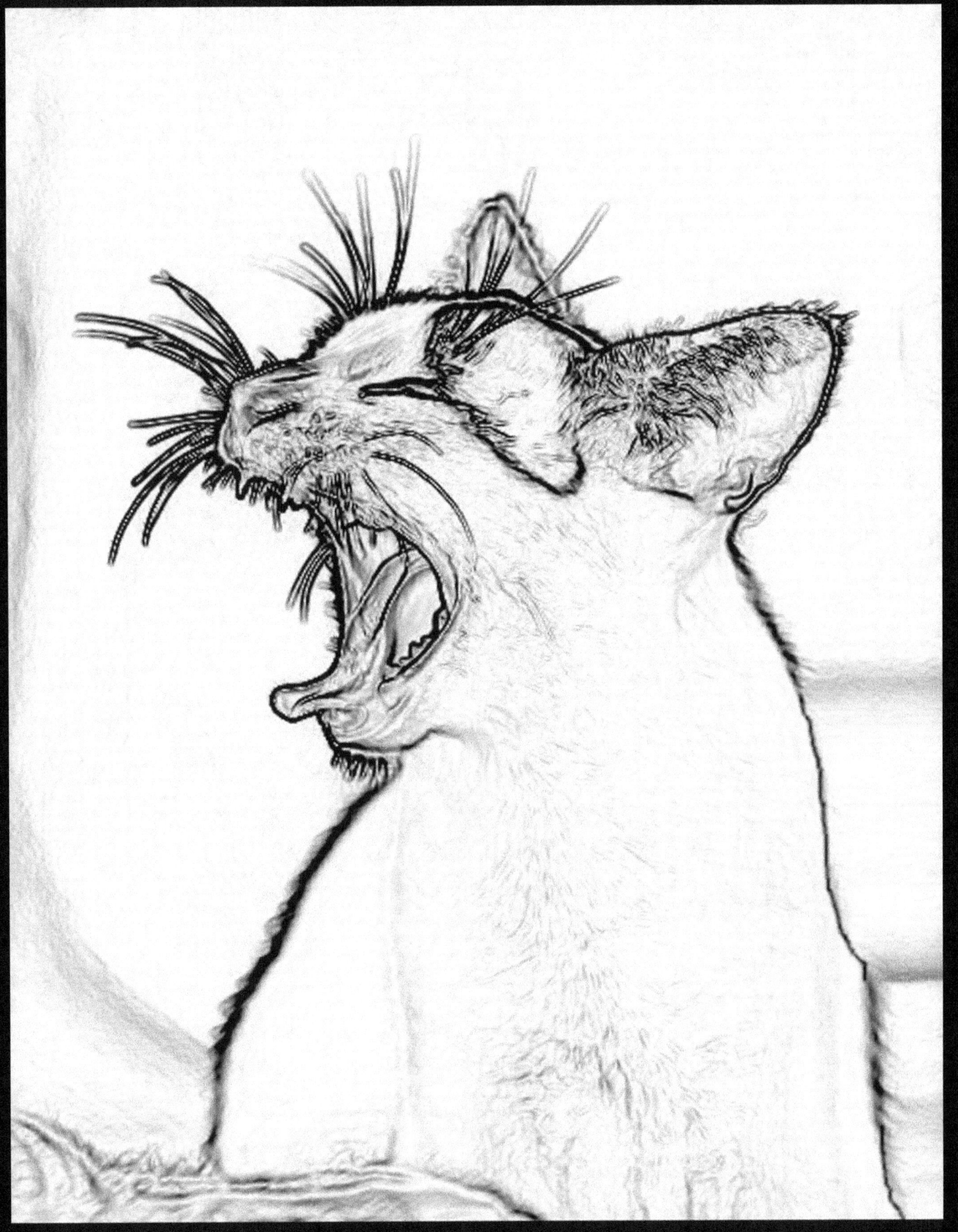

What's your kitty's favorite color?

Purr-ple!

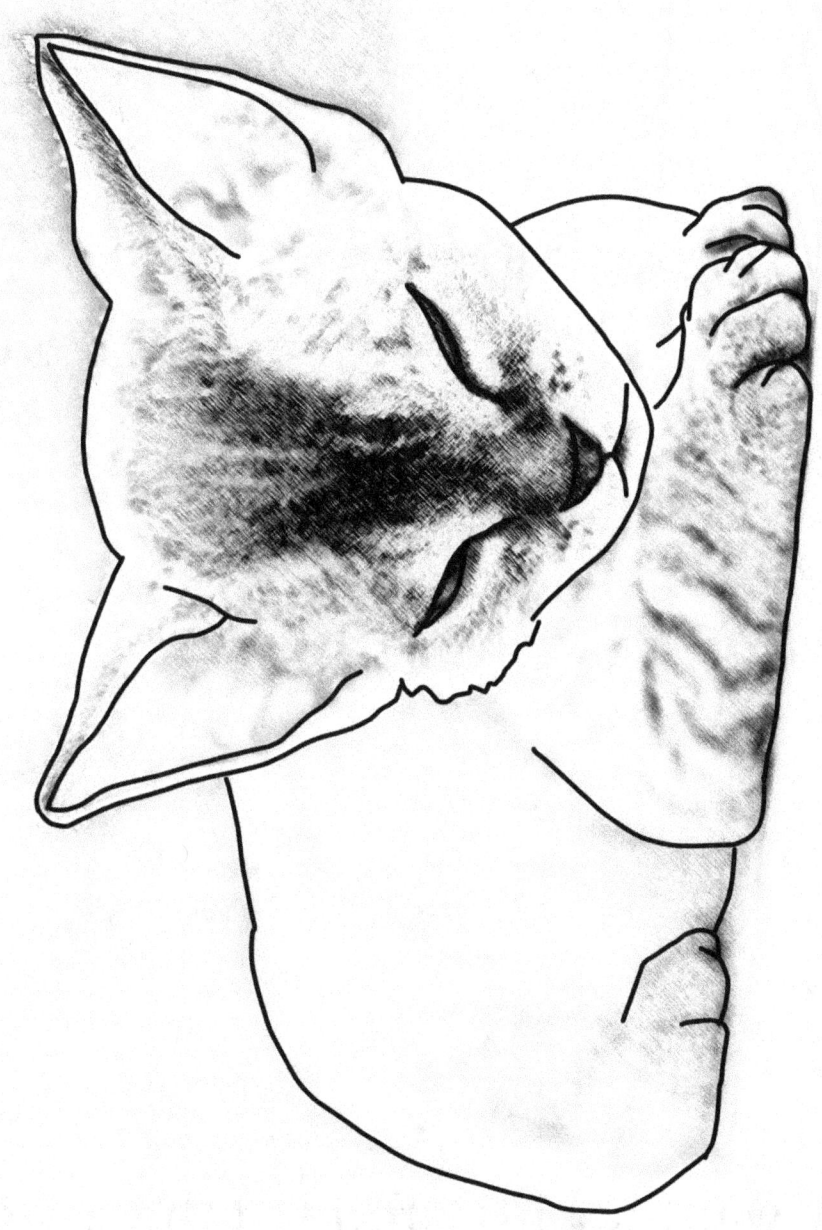

Why was the kitty afraid of the tree?

Because of it's bark!

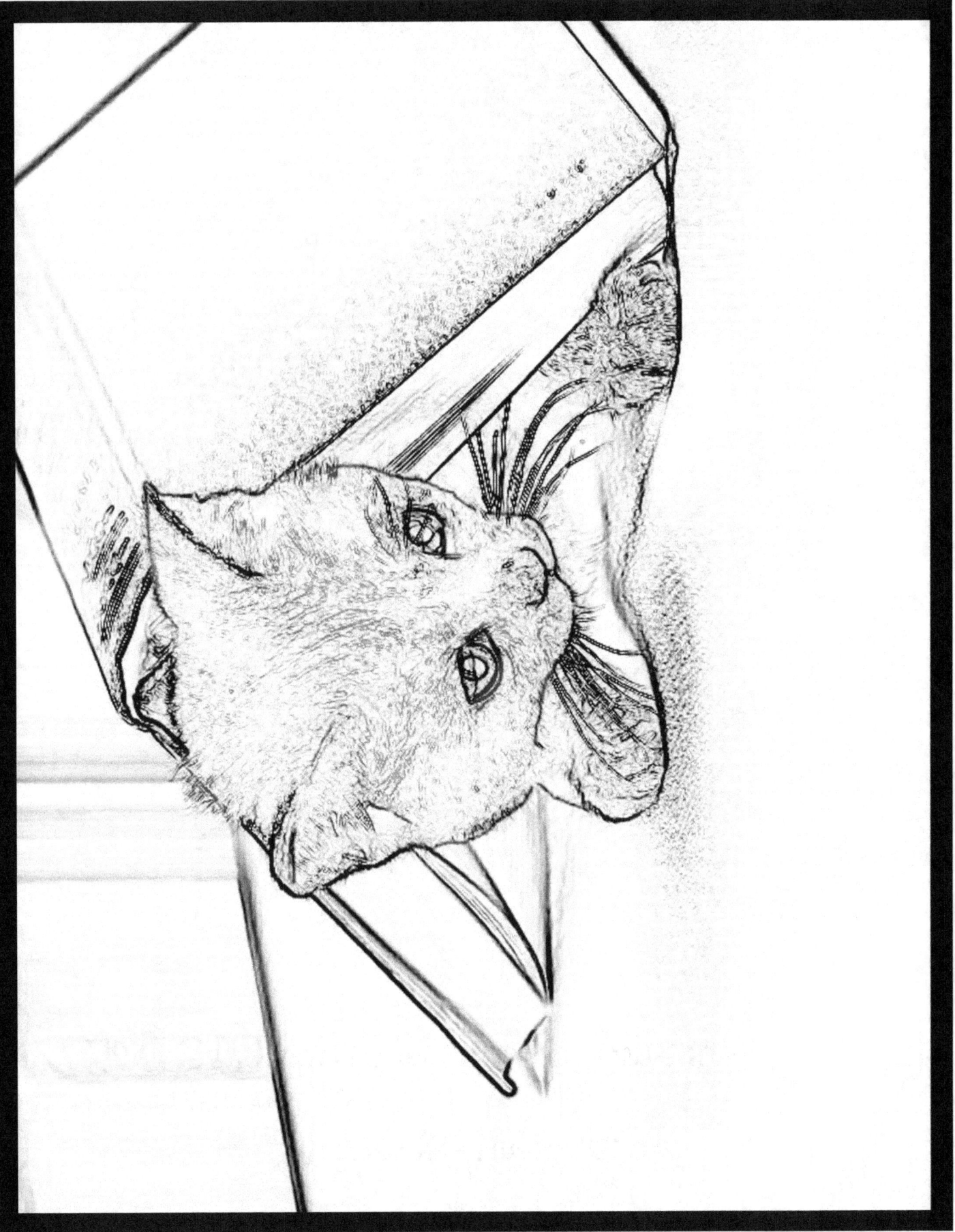

What did the confused kitty say?

"I'm purr-plexed!"

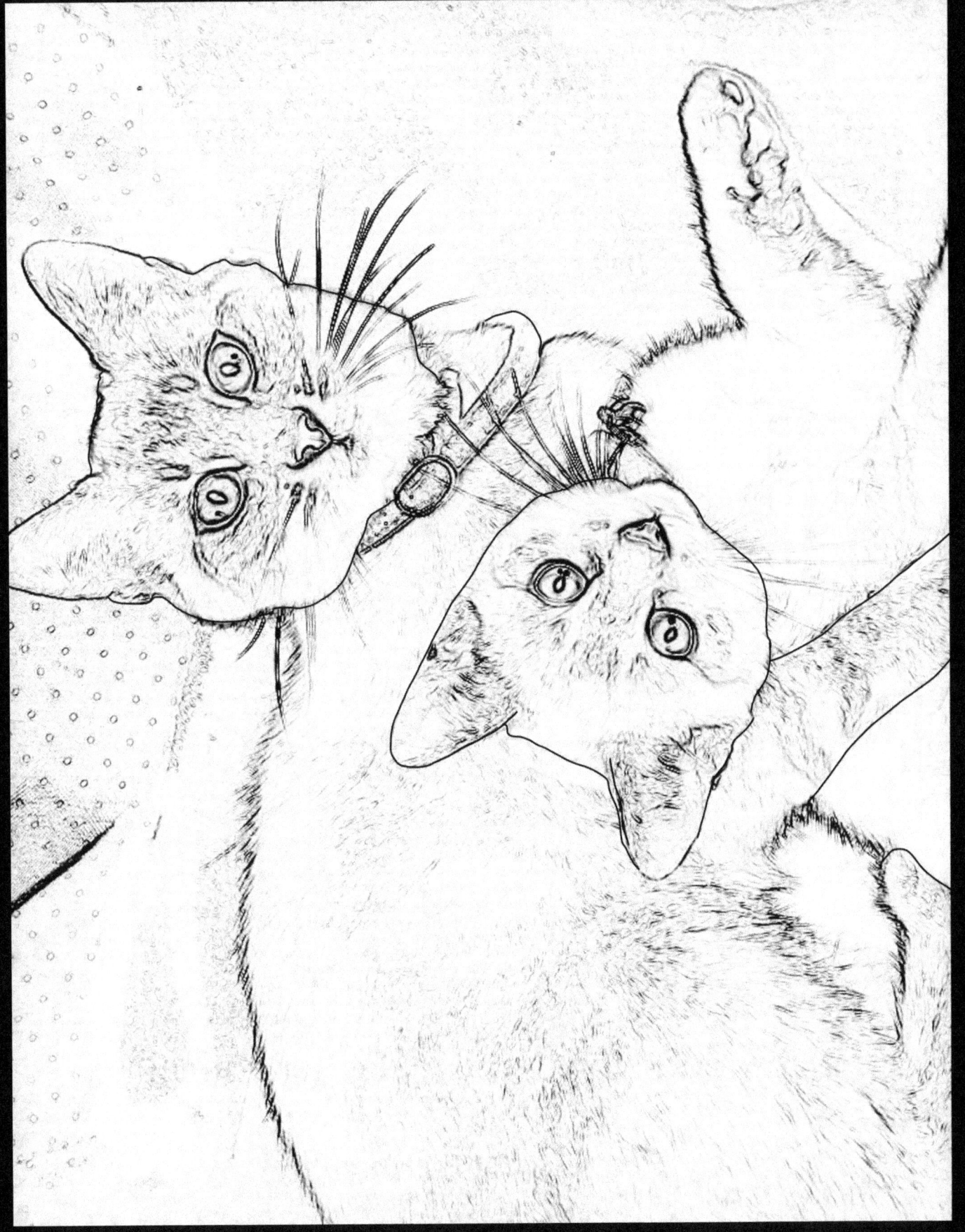

How does your kitty make her coffee?

She lets it purr-colate!

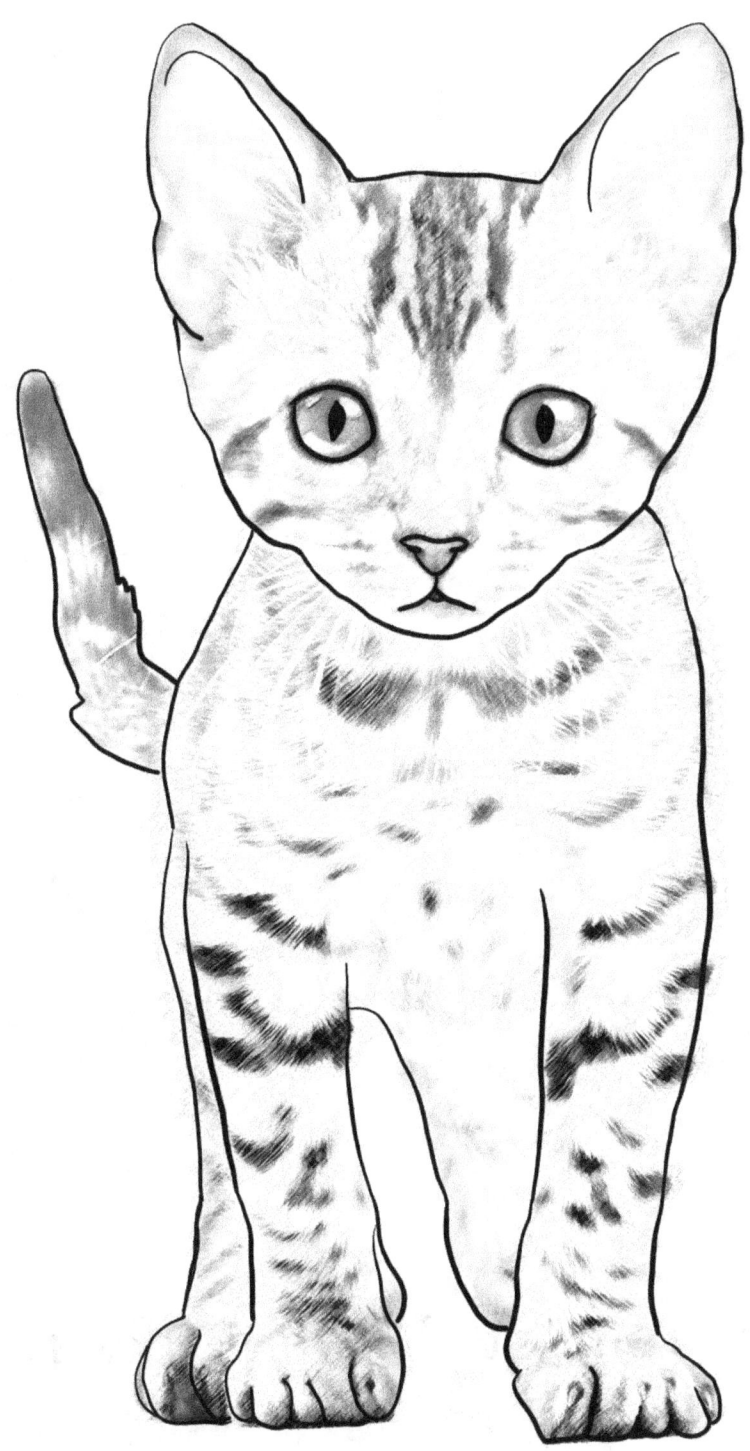

What's your kitty's favorite desert?

Chocolate Mouse!

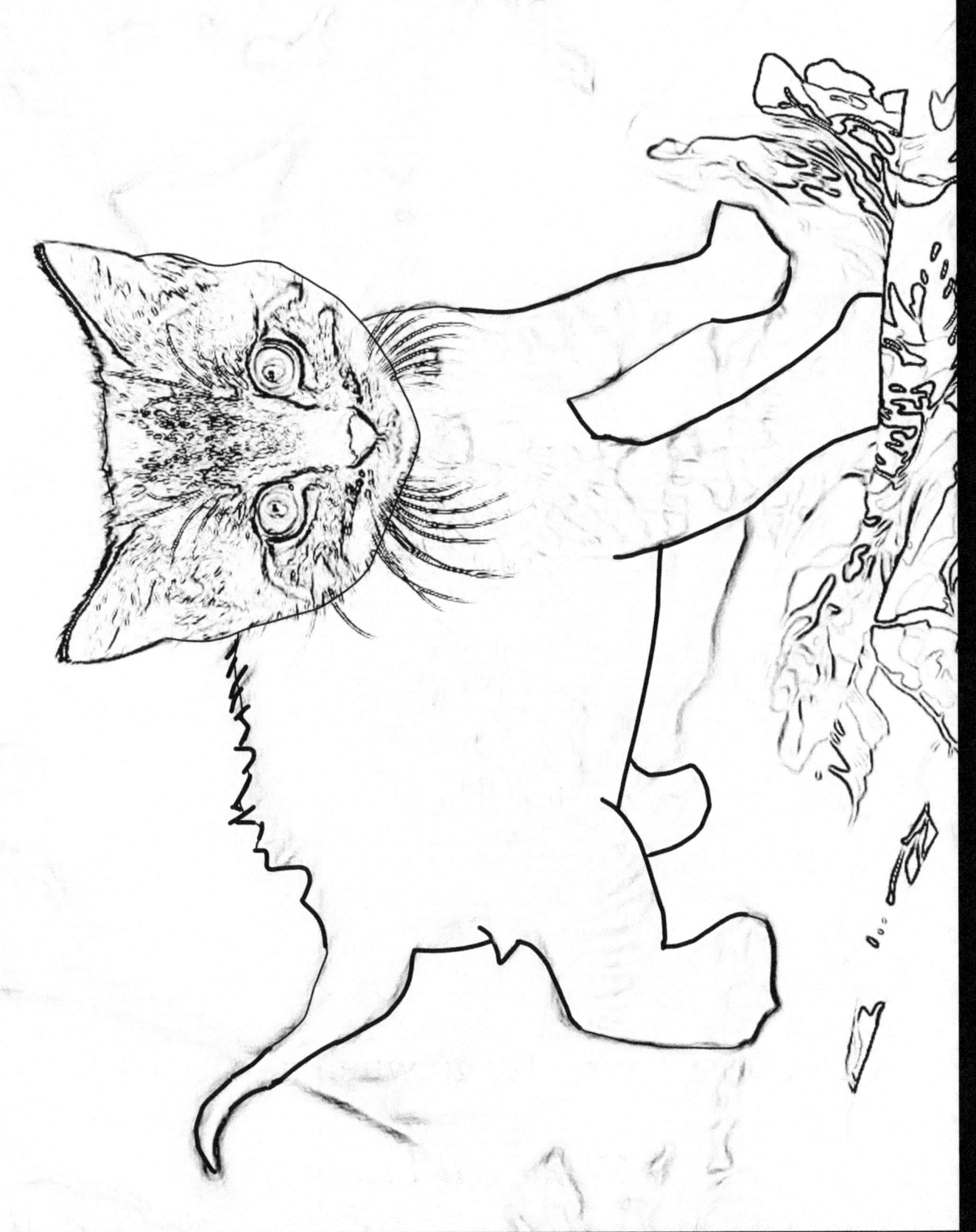

Where does your kitty go when it loses it's tail?

To the retail store!

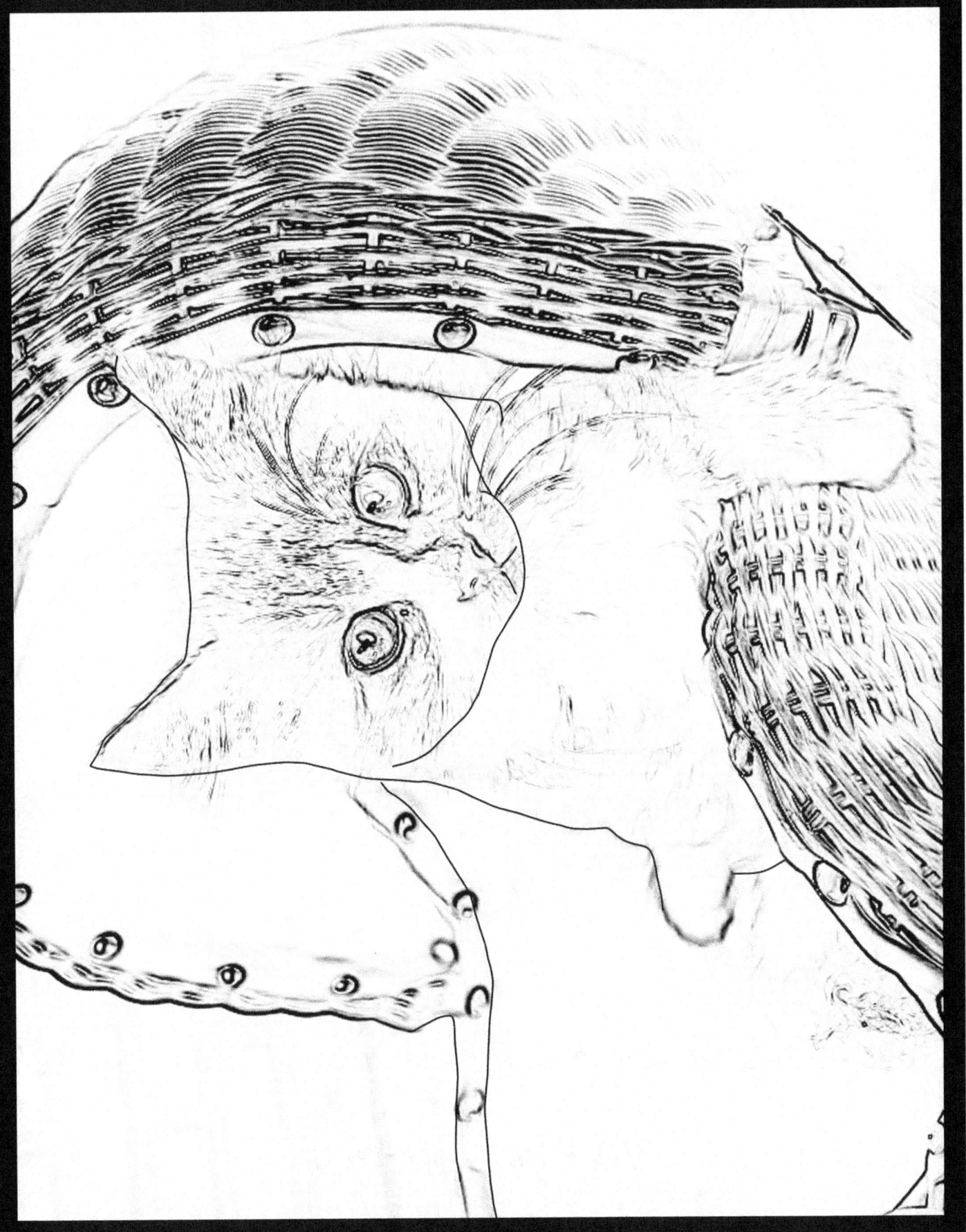

Does your kitty demand any of your business profits?

Yes - fifty purr-cent!

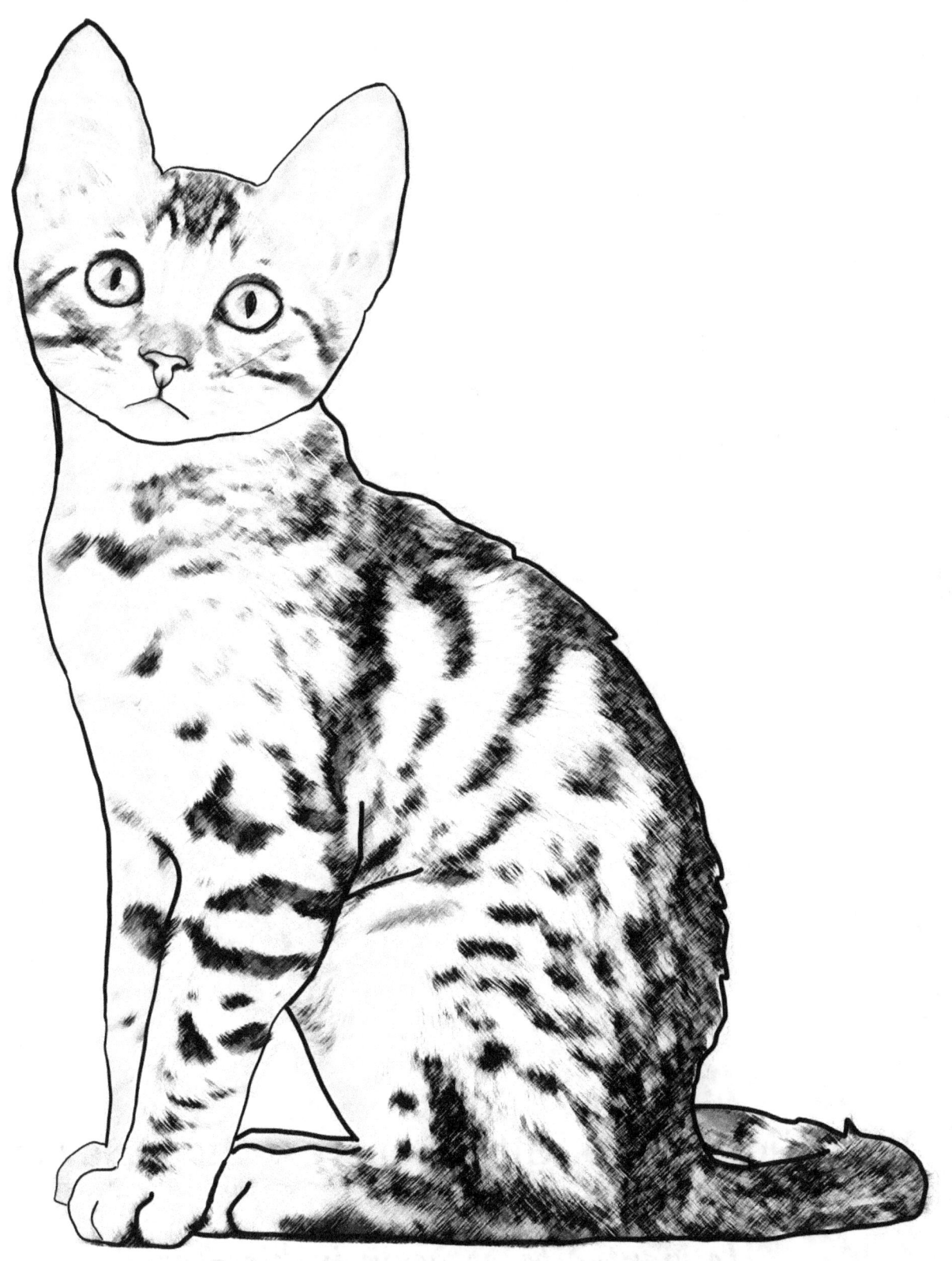

Why did George Kittenton cross the Delaware?

He wanted to go down in hiss-tory!

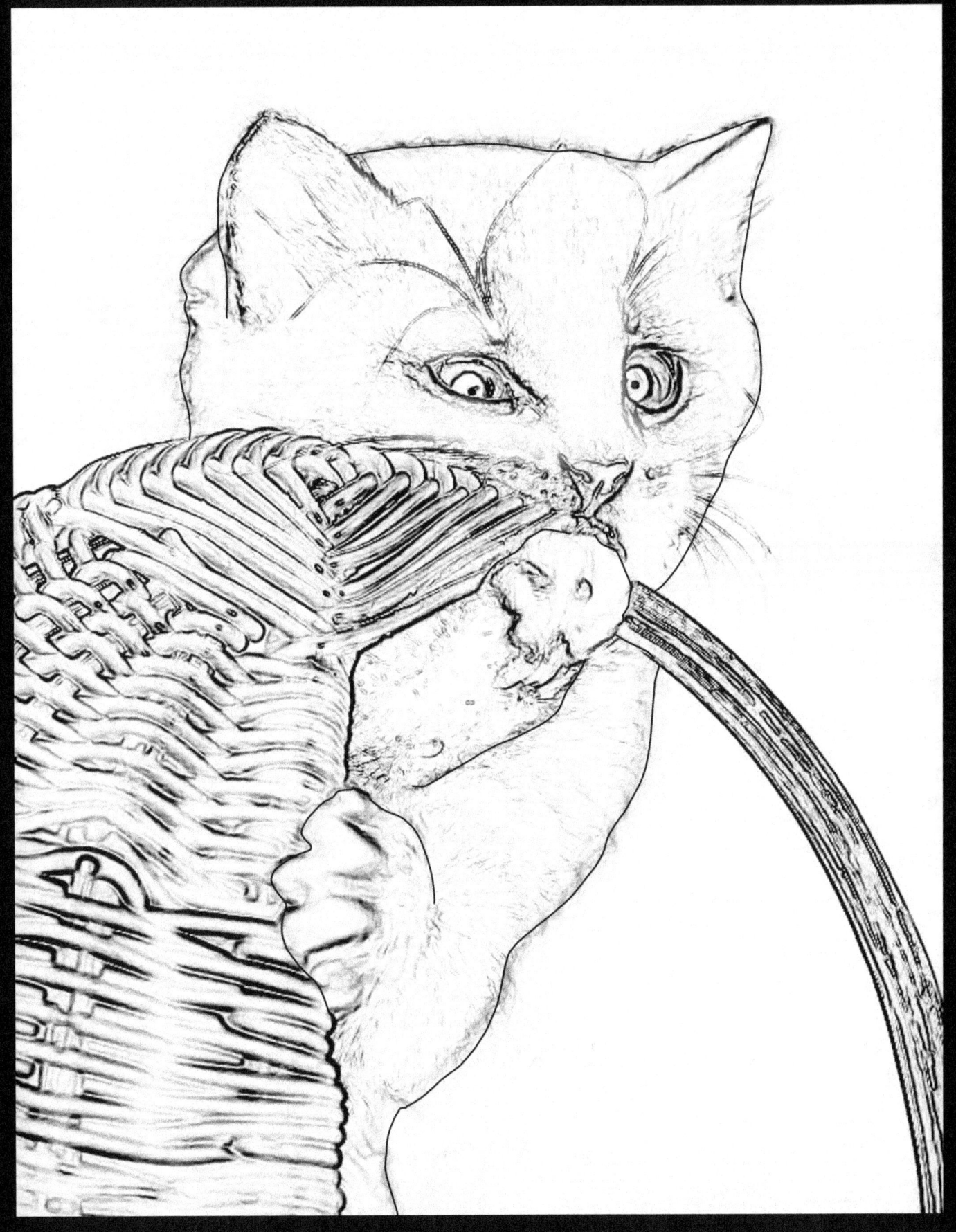

What do you call a kitty who lives in an igloo?

An Eski-mew!

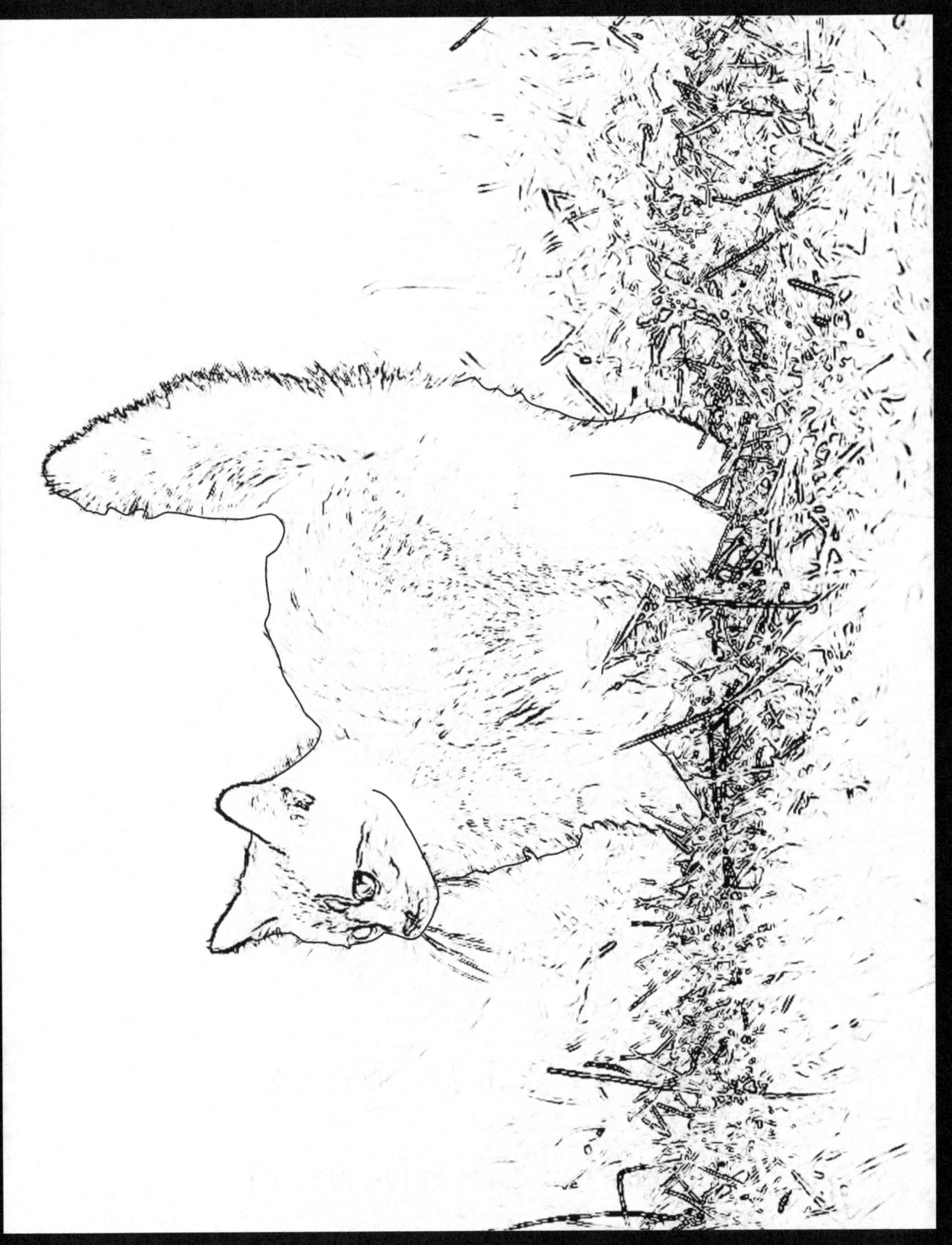

How do kitties stop crime?

They call claw enforcement!

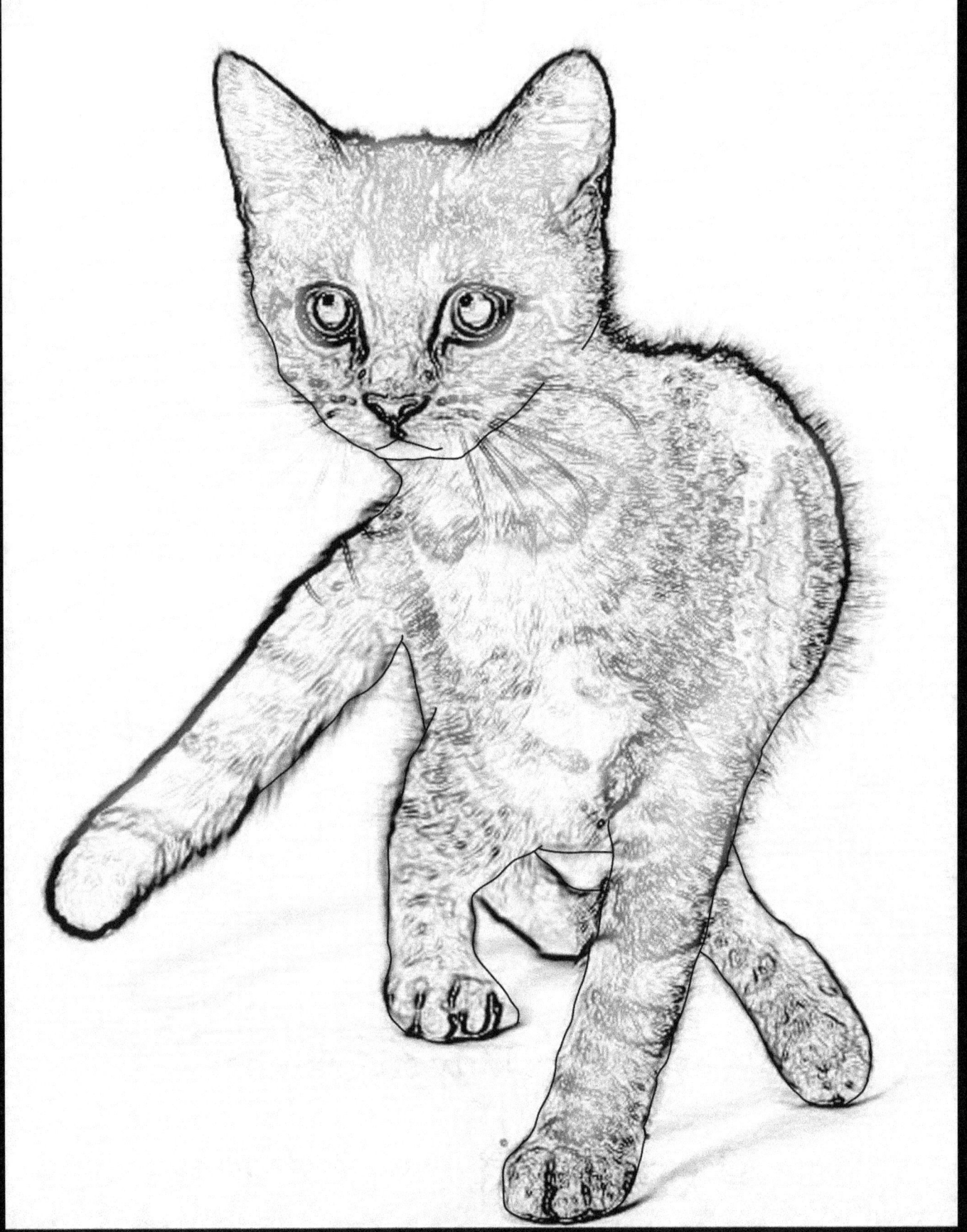

Why was the kitty so grumpy?

Because she was in a bad mewd!

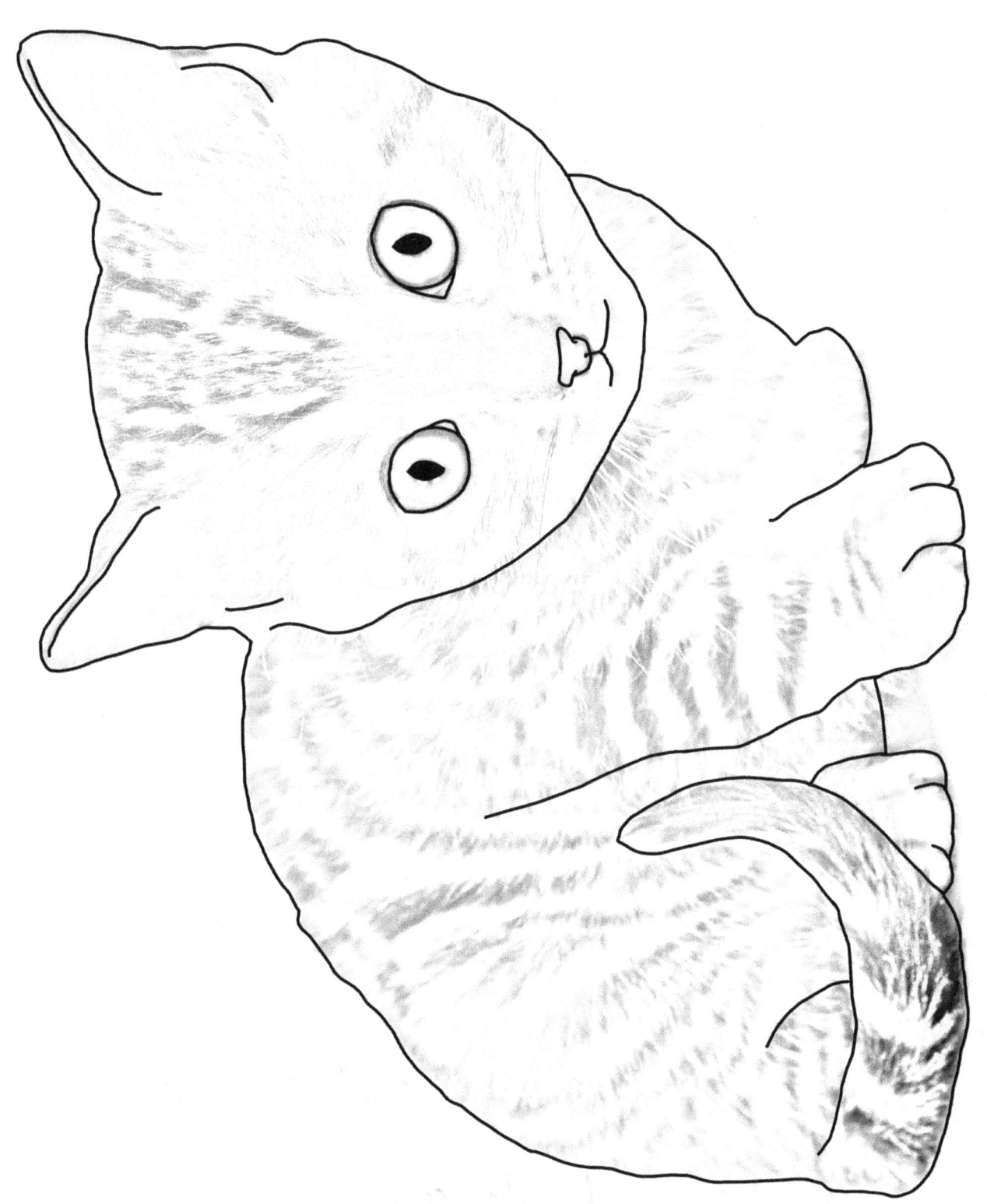

What do you call a kitty who loves to bowl?

An alley cat!

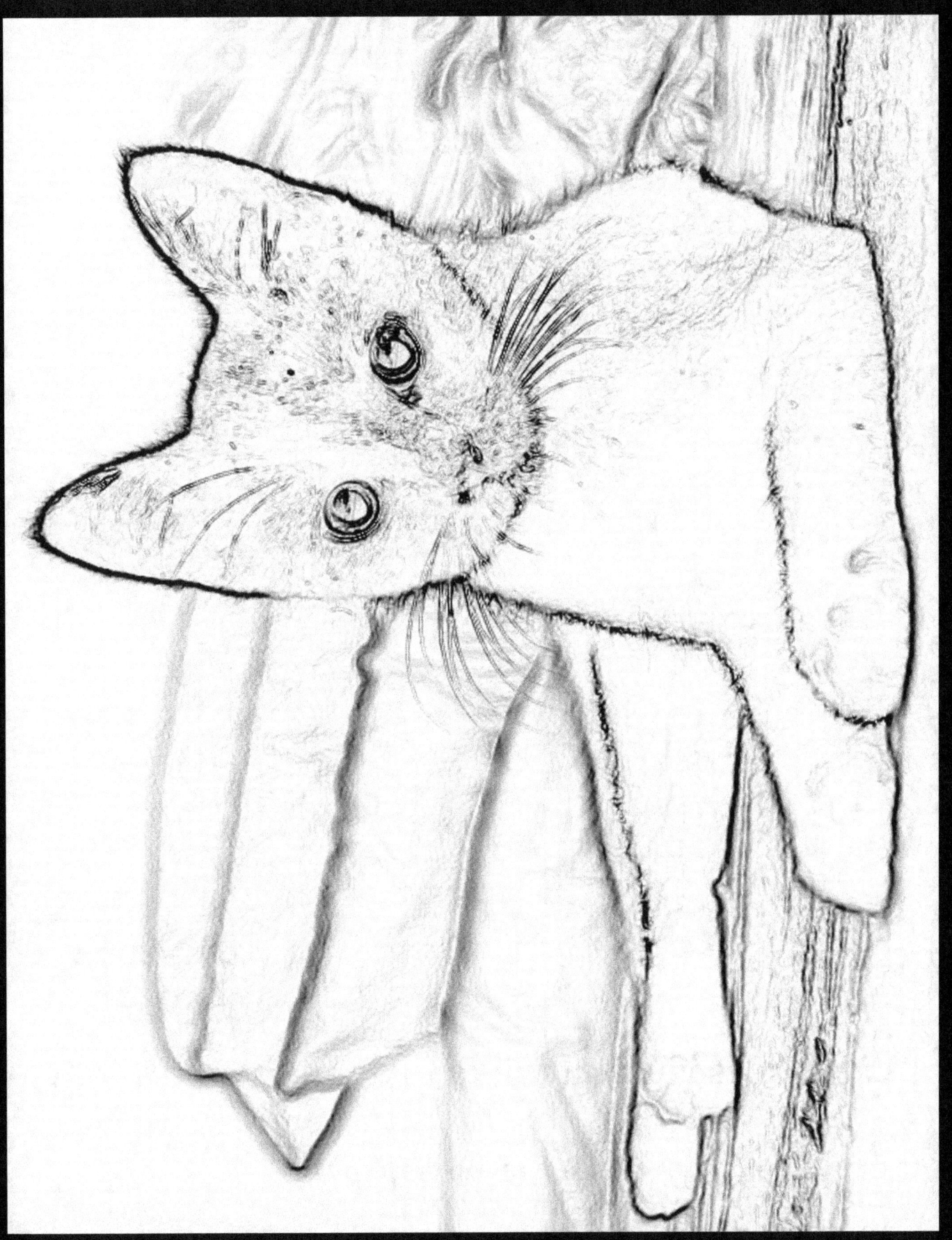

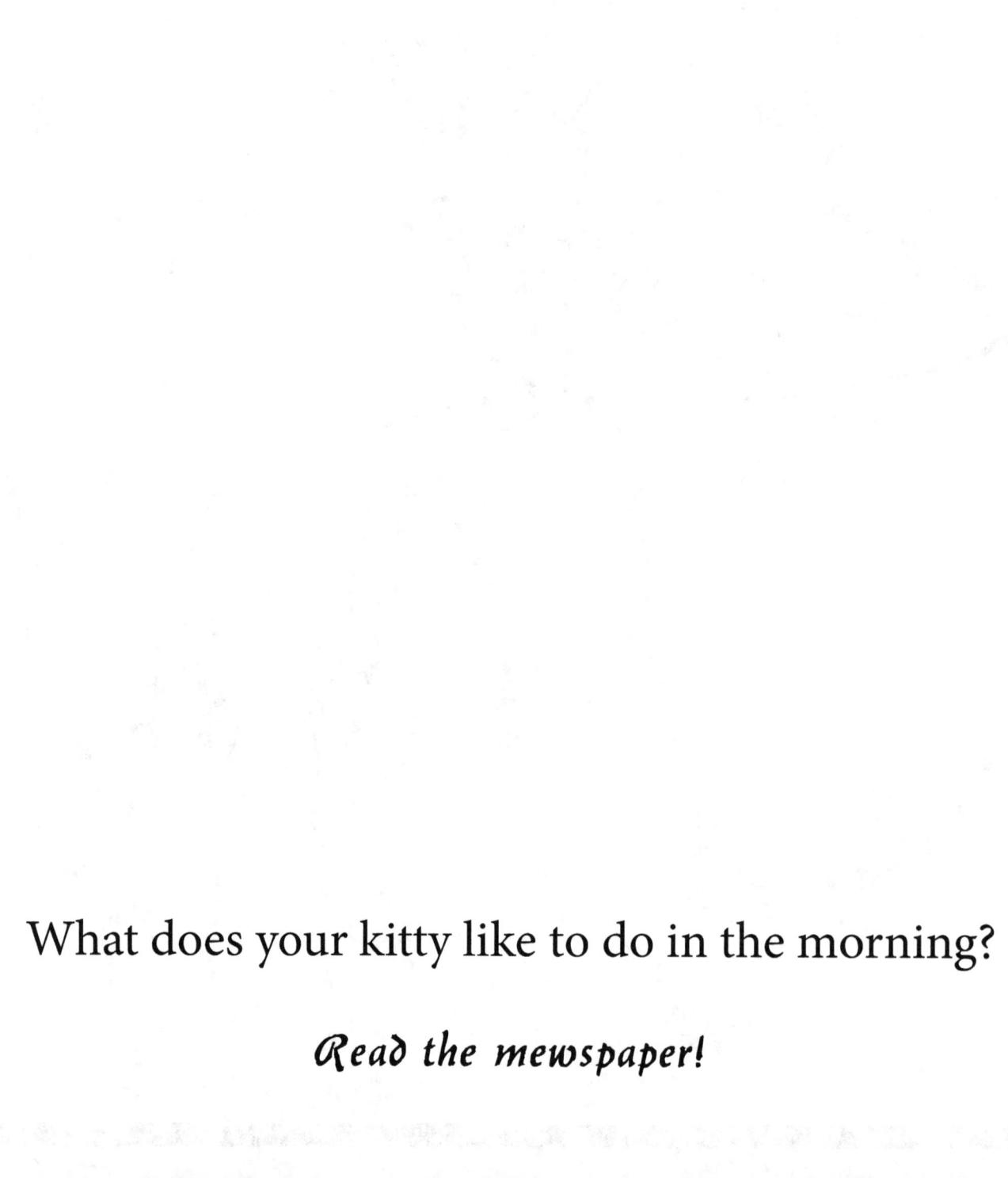

What does your kitty like to do in the morning?

Read the mewspaper!

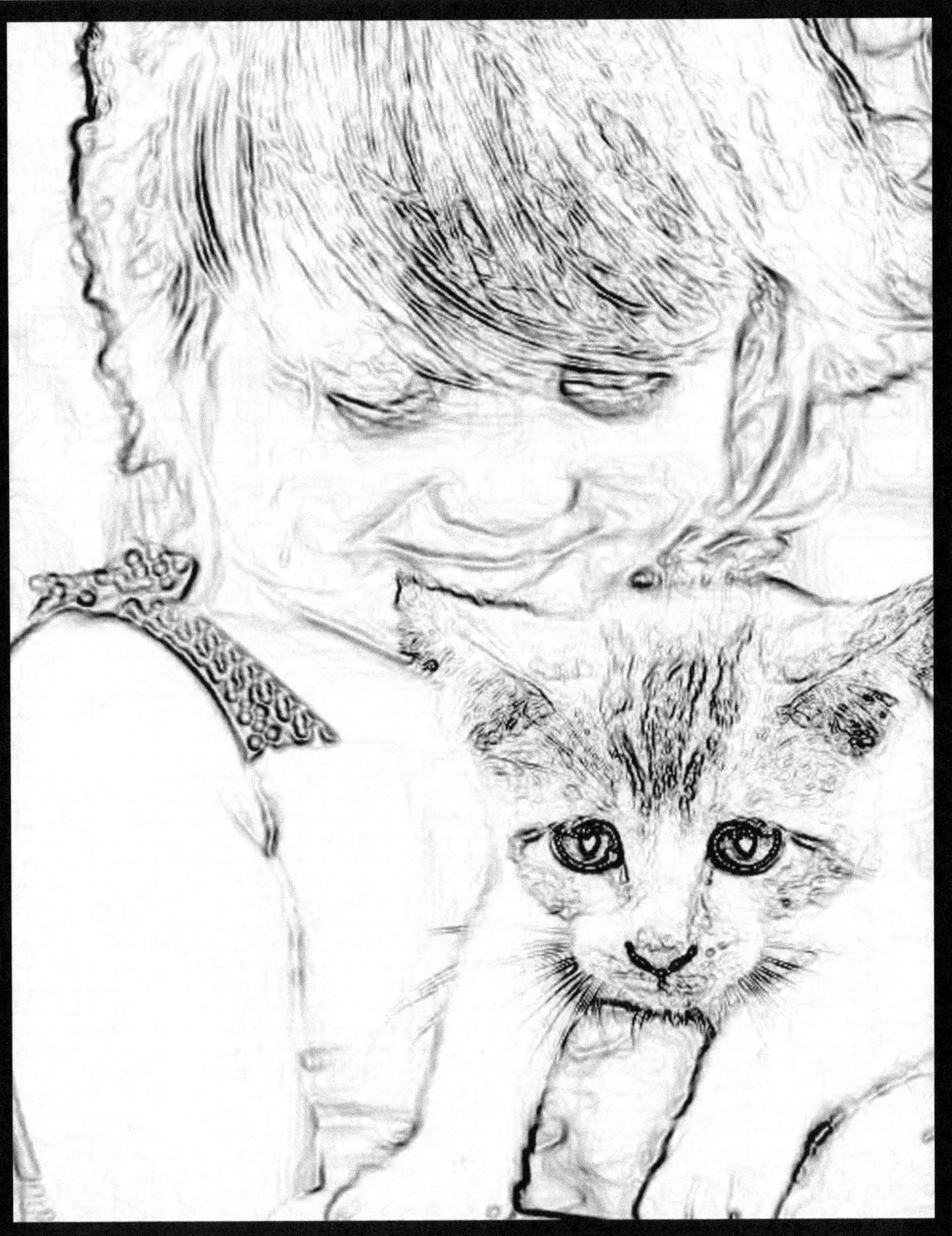

How is your kitty's food sold?

Purr the can!

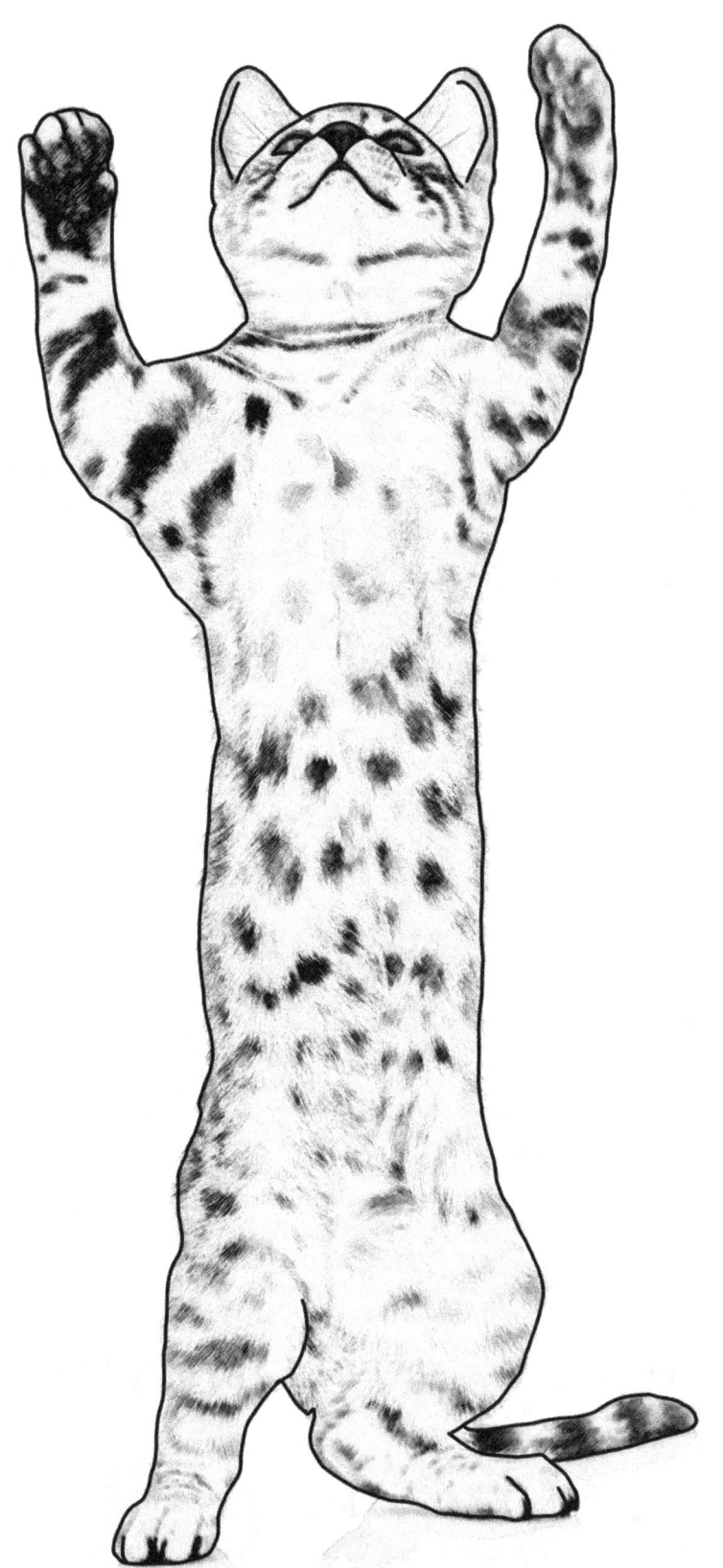

What do baby kittens wear?

Diapurrs!

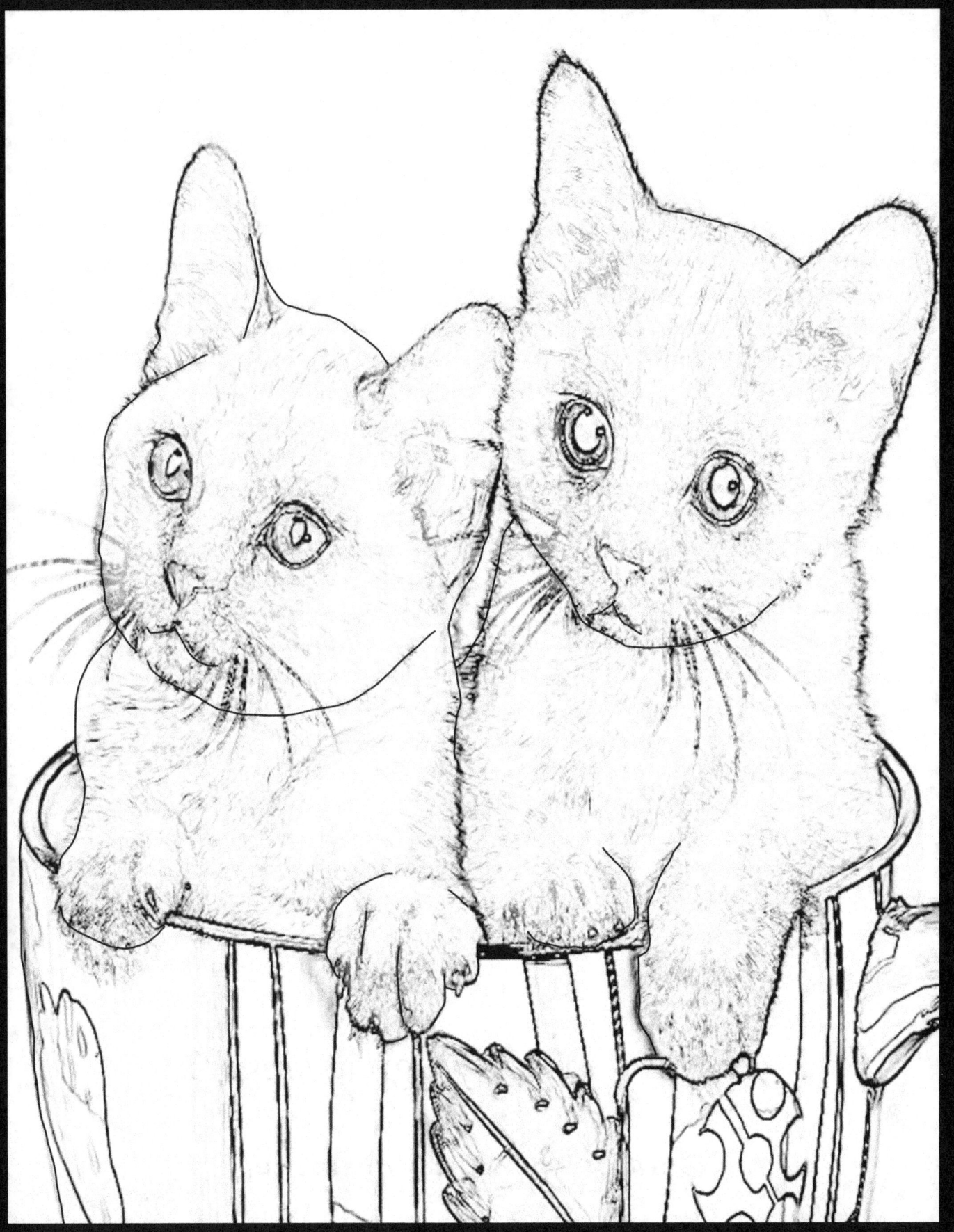

Why is your kitty a great singer?

Because she's very mewsical!

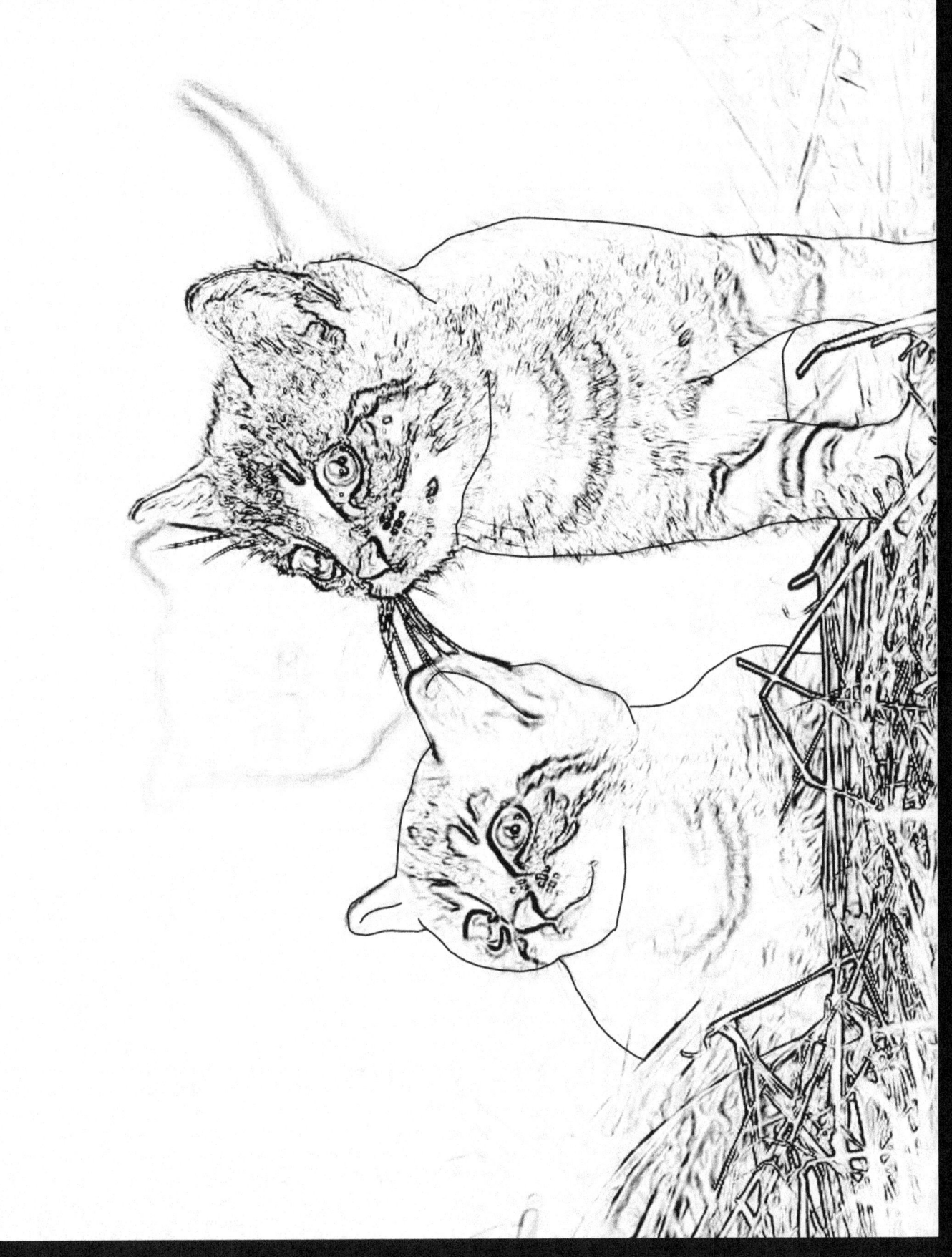

Why can't kitties play cards in the jungle?

There are too many cheetahs!

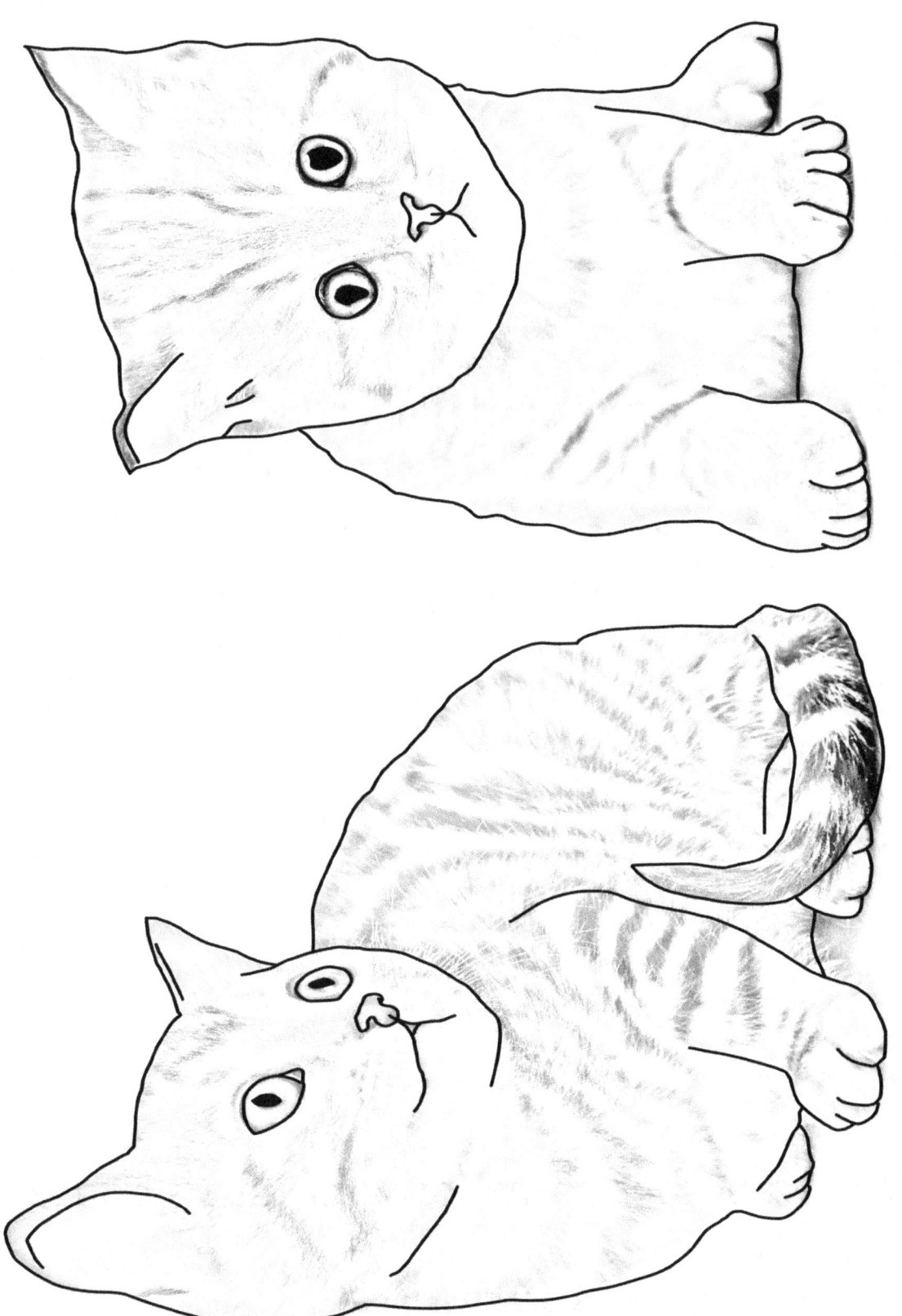

What's another name for your kitty's house?

A scratch pad!

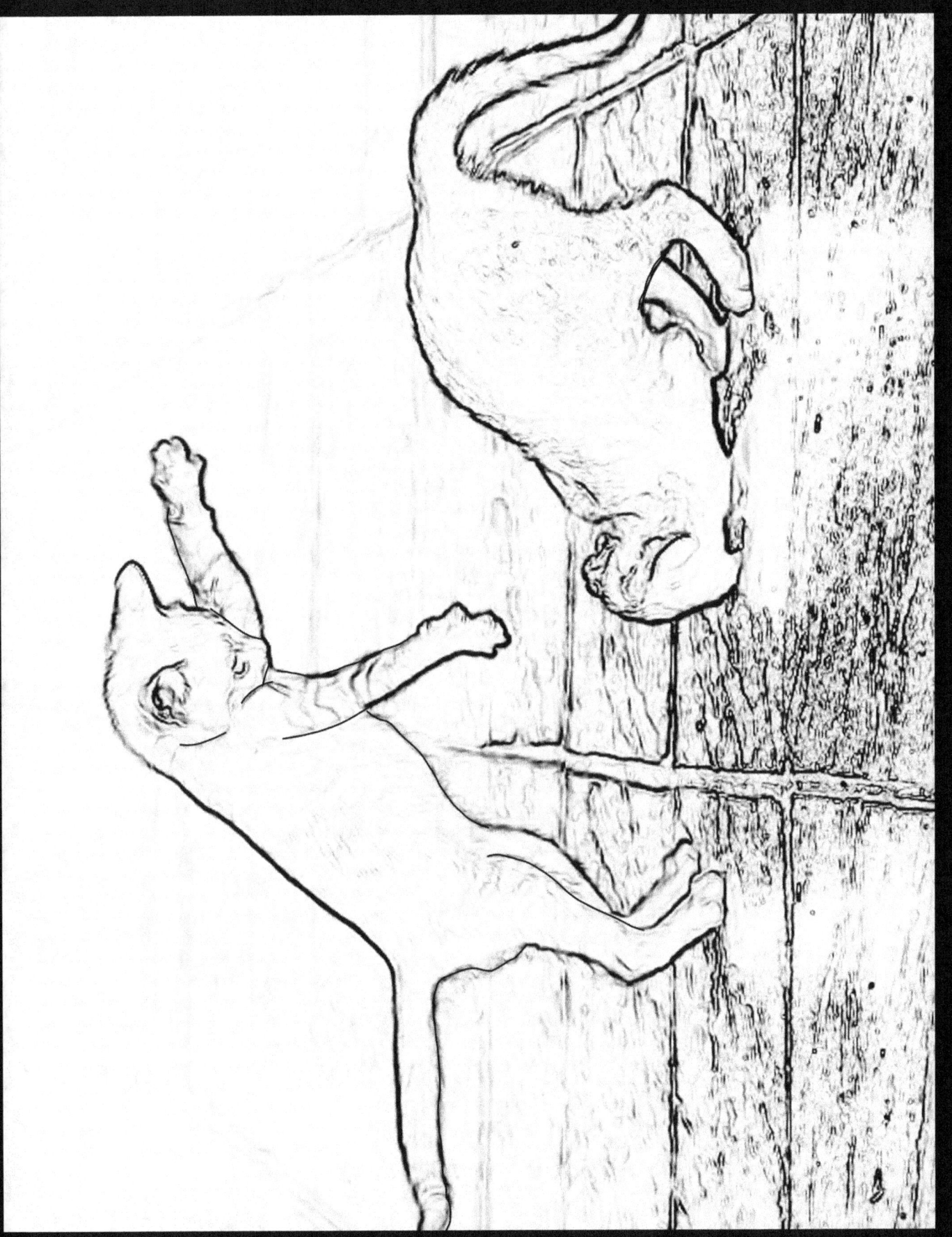

What should you say to your kitty when you leave?

Have a mice day!

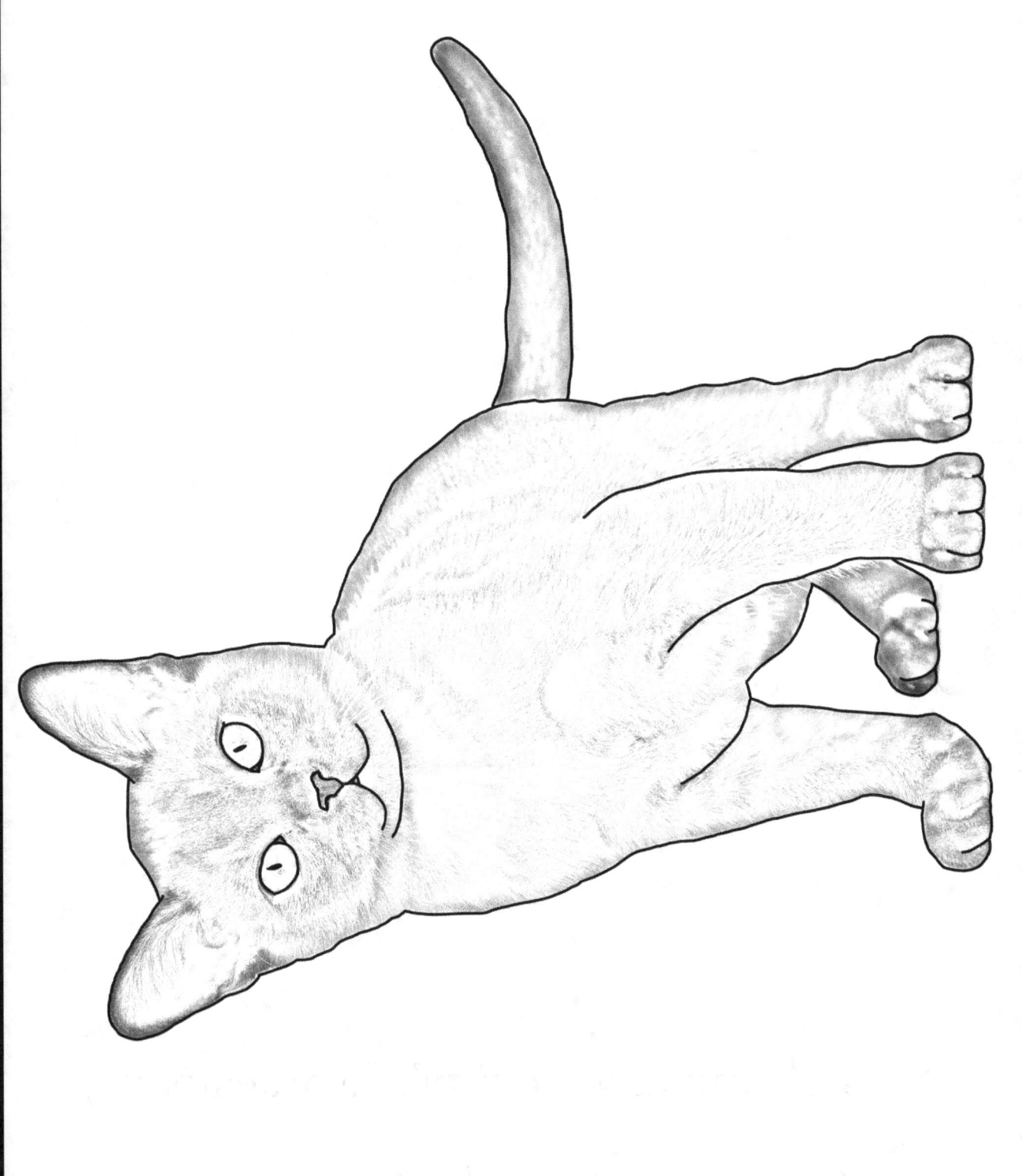

Why is Christmas your kitty's favorite holiday?

She likes waiting up for Santa Claws!

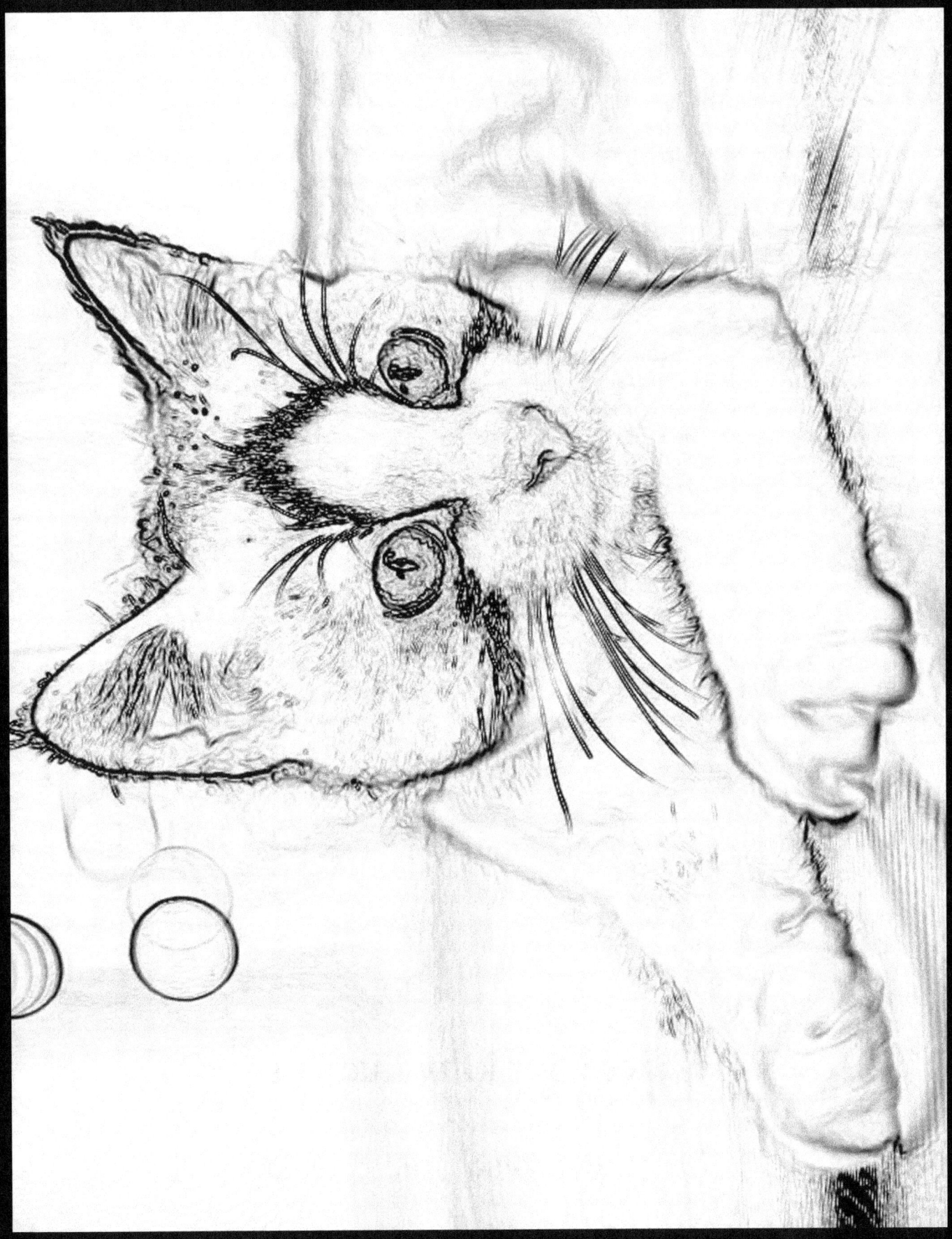

How does your kitty like to shop?

She flips through the cat-alog!

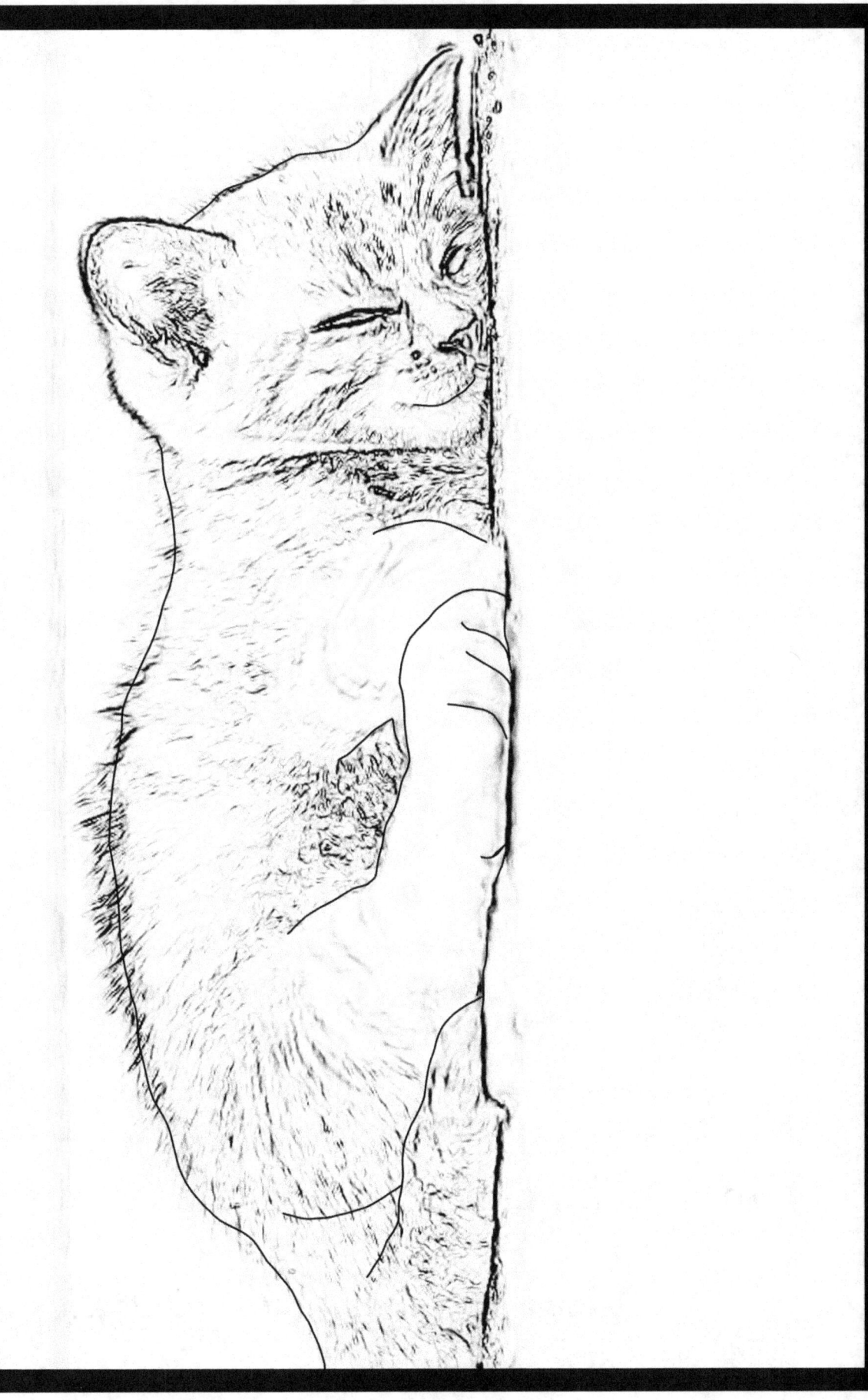

In what kind of weather is the vet busiest?

When it's raining cats and dogs!

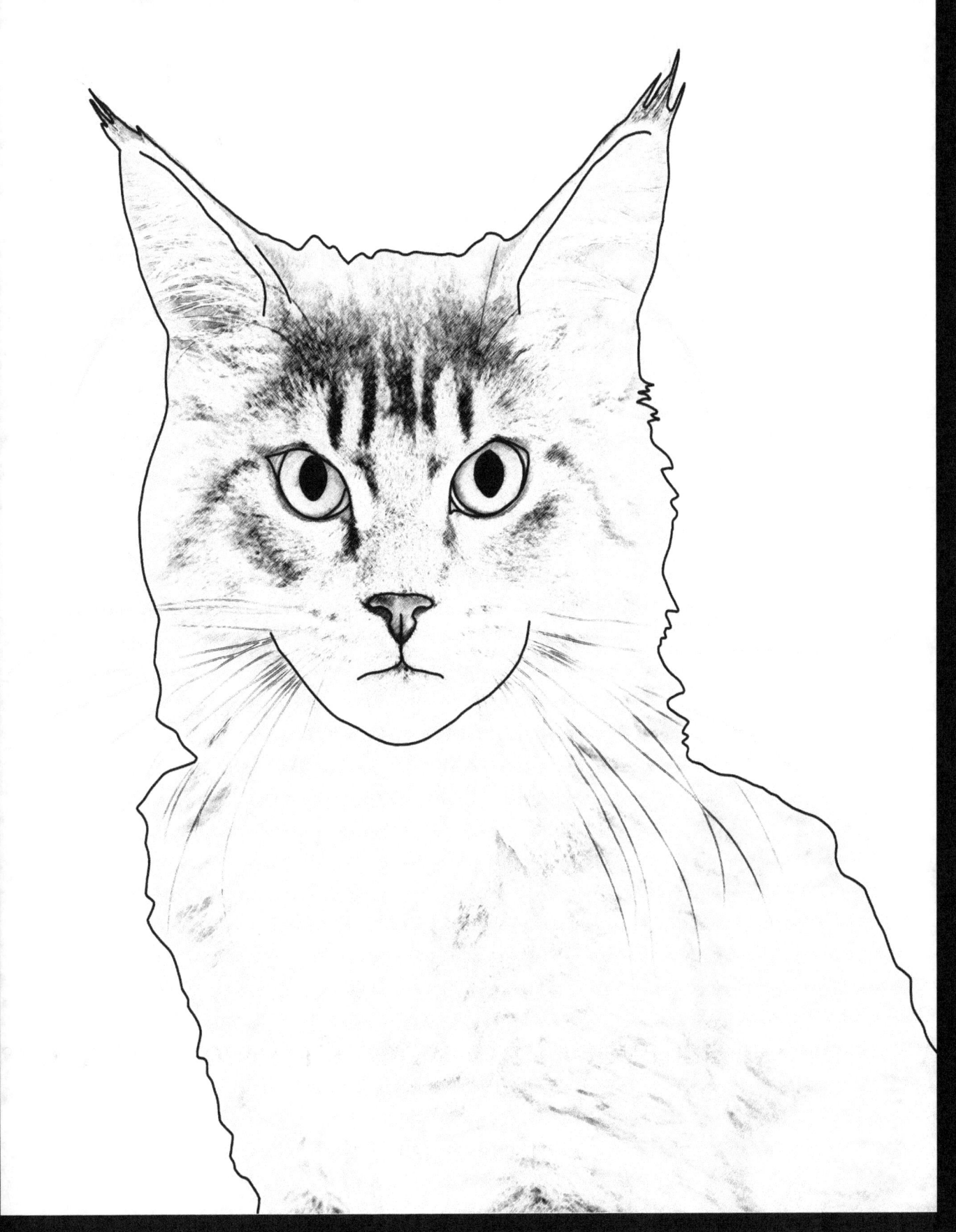

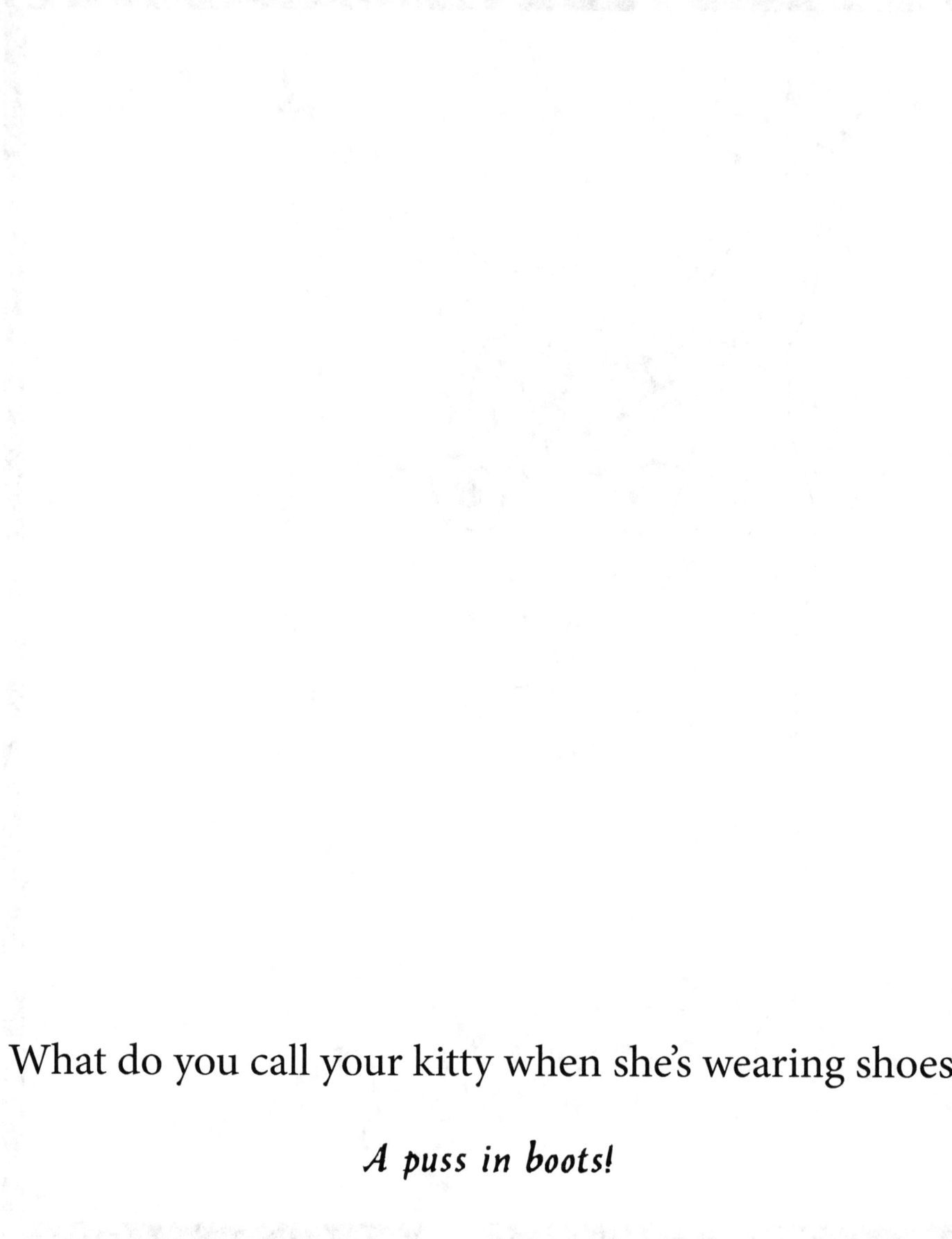

What do you call your kitty when she's wearing shoes?

A puss in boots!

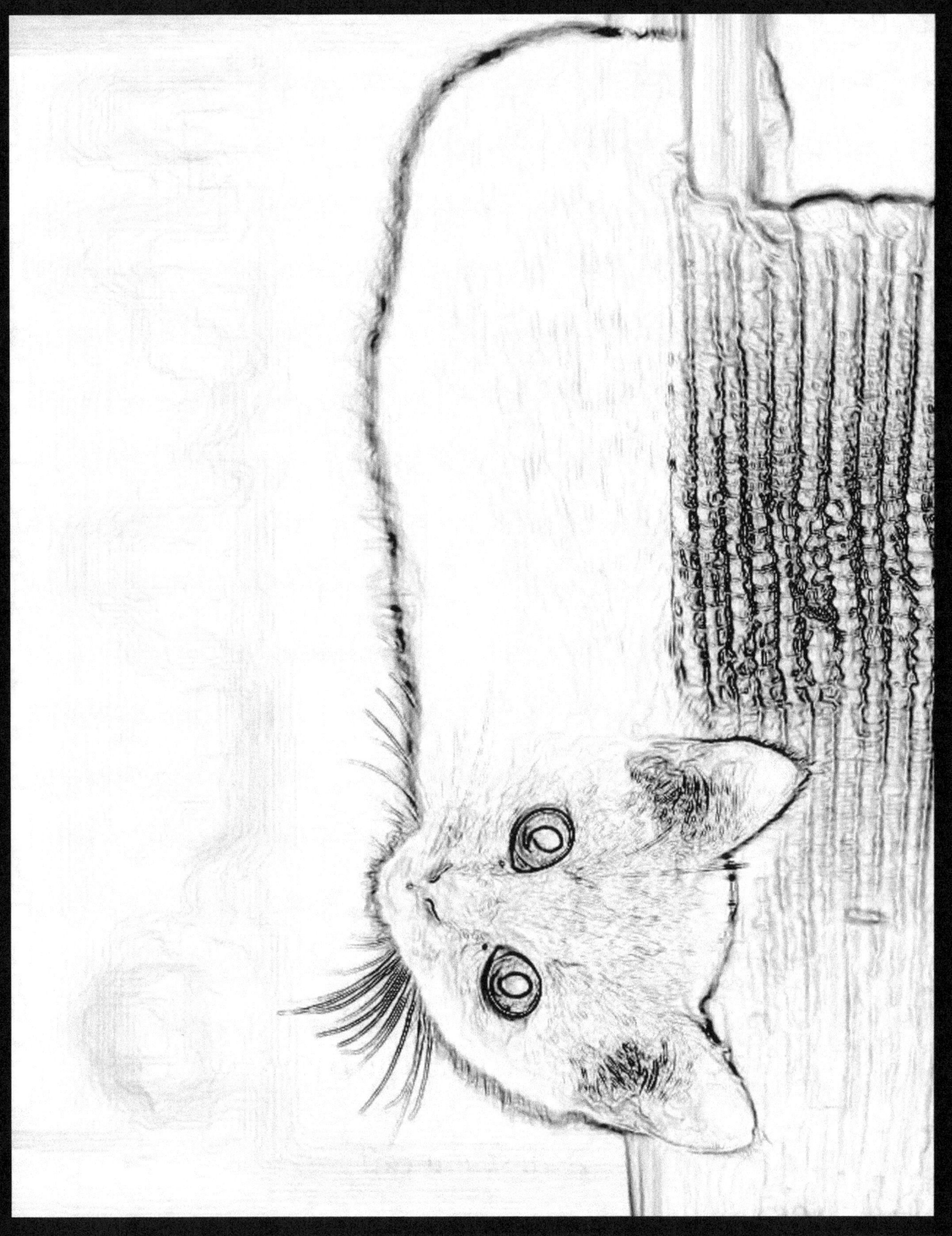

What type of kitty works for the Red Cross?

A first aid cat!

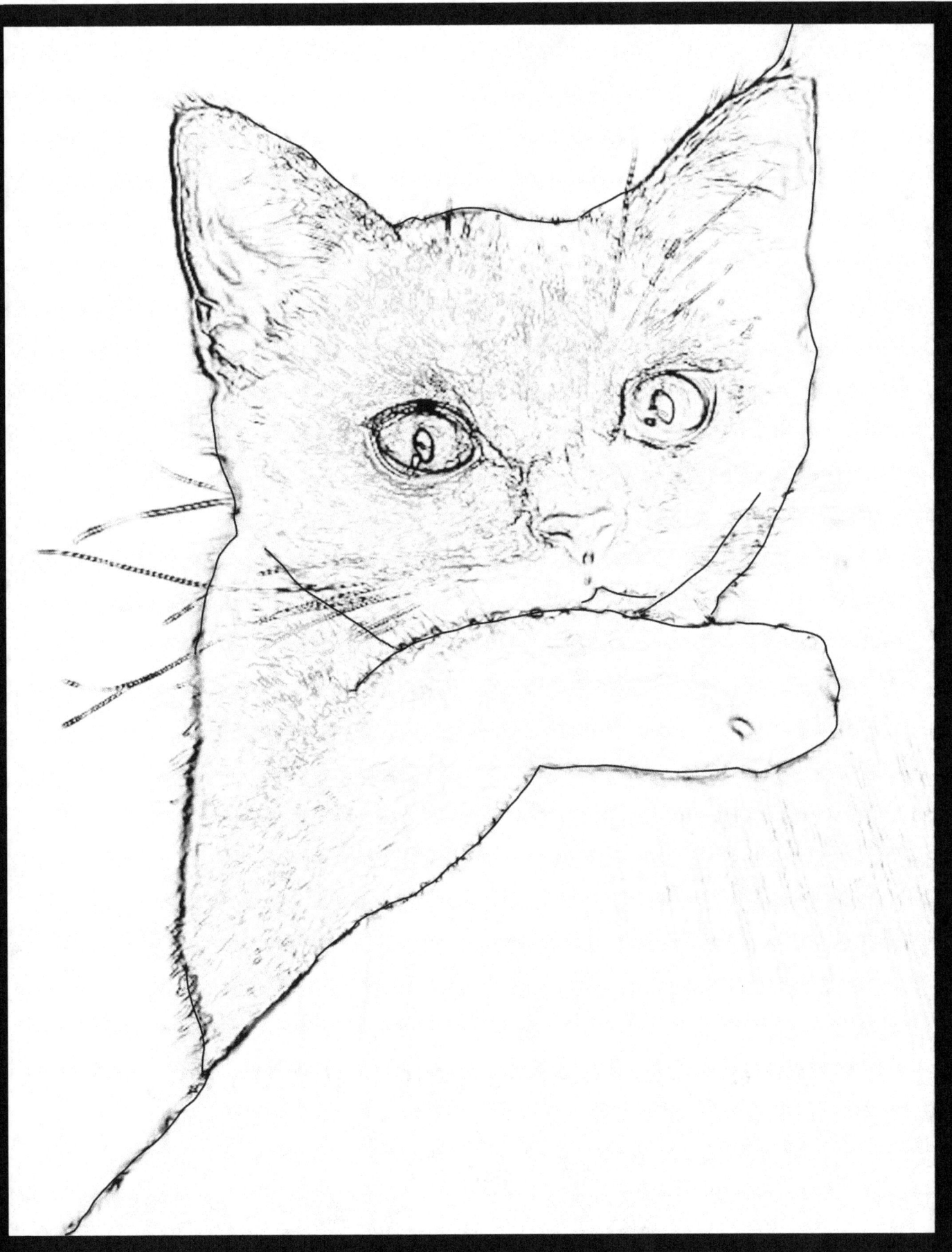

What do you call a kitty in a station wagon?

A car-pet!

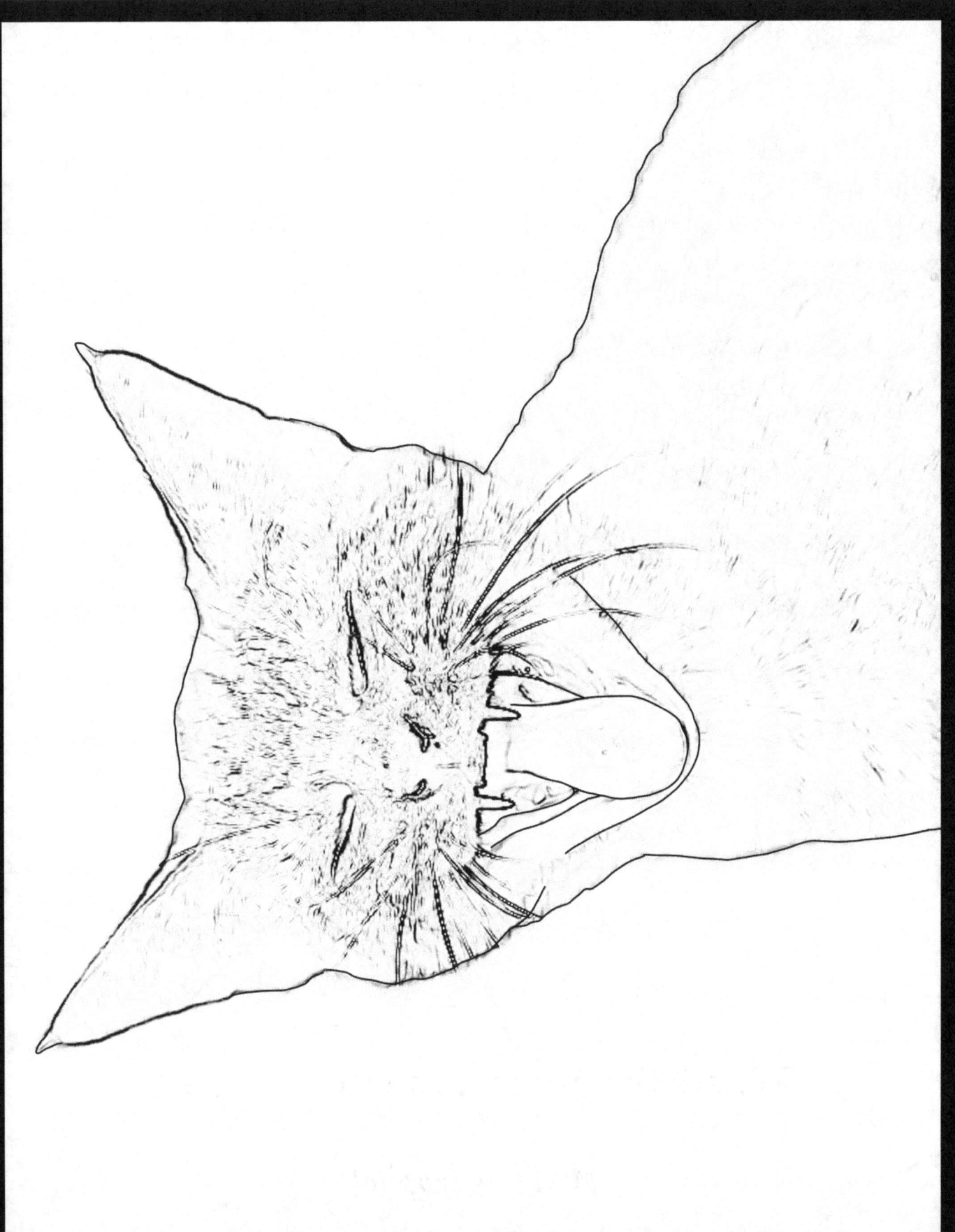

What's the unluckiest kitty to have?

A cat-astrophe!

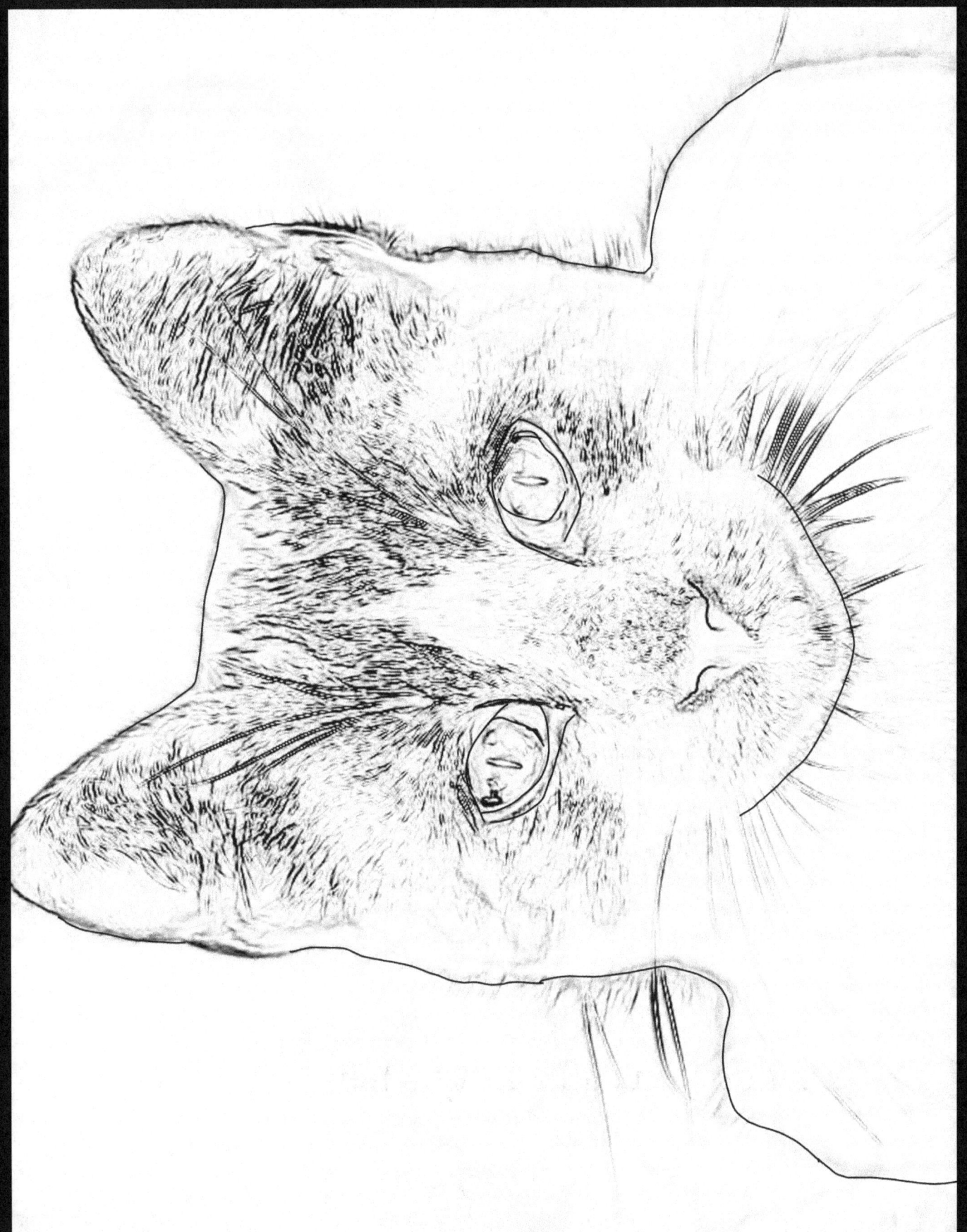

What do you call a kitty when he gets old?

Grand-paw!

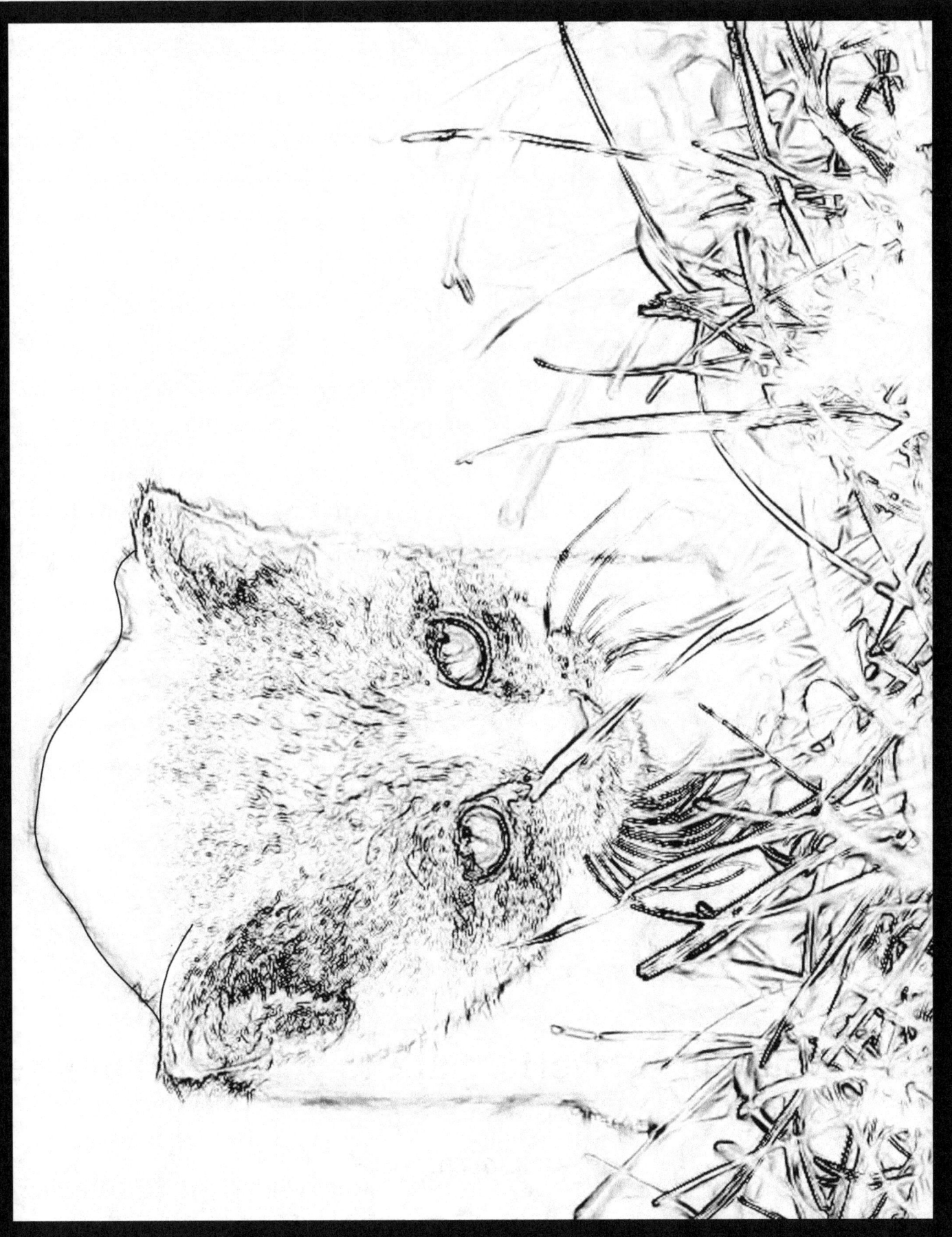

What's your kitty's favorite game to play with a mouse?

Catch!

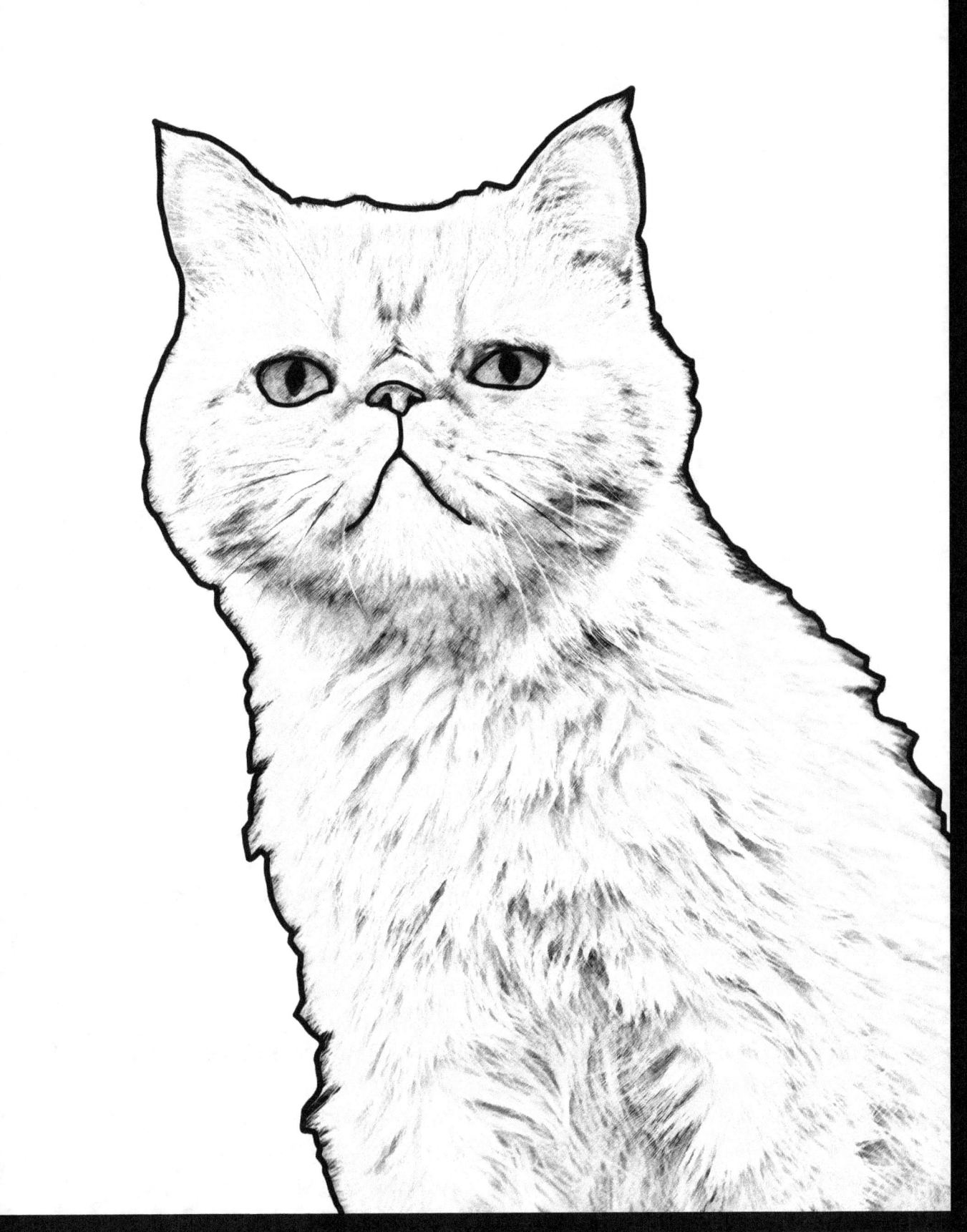

Why did the kitty have trouble with the DVD?

Turns out it was on paws!

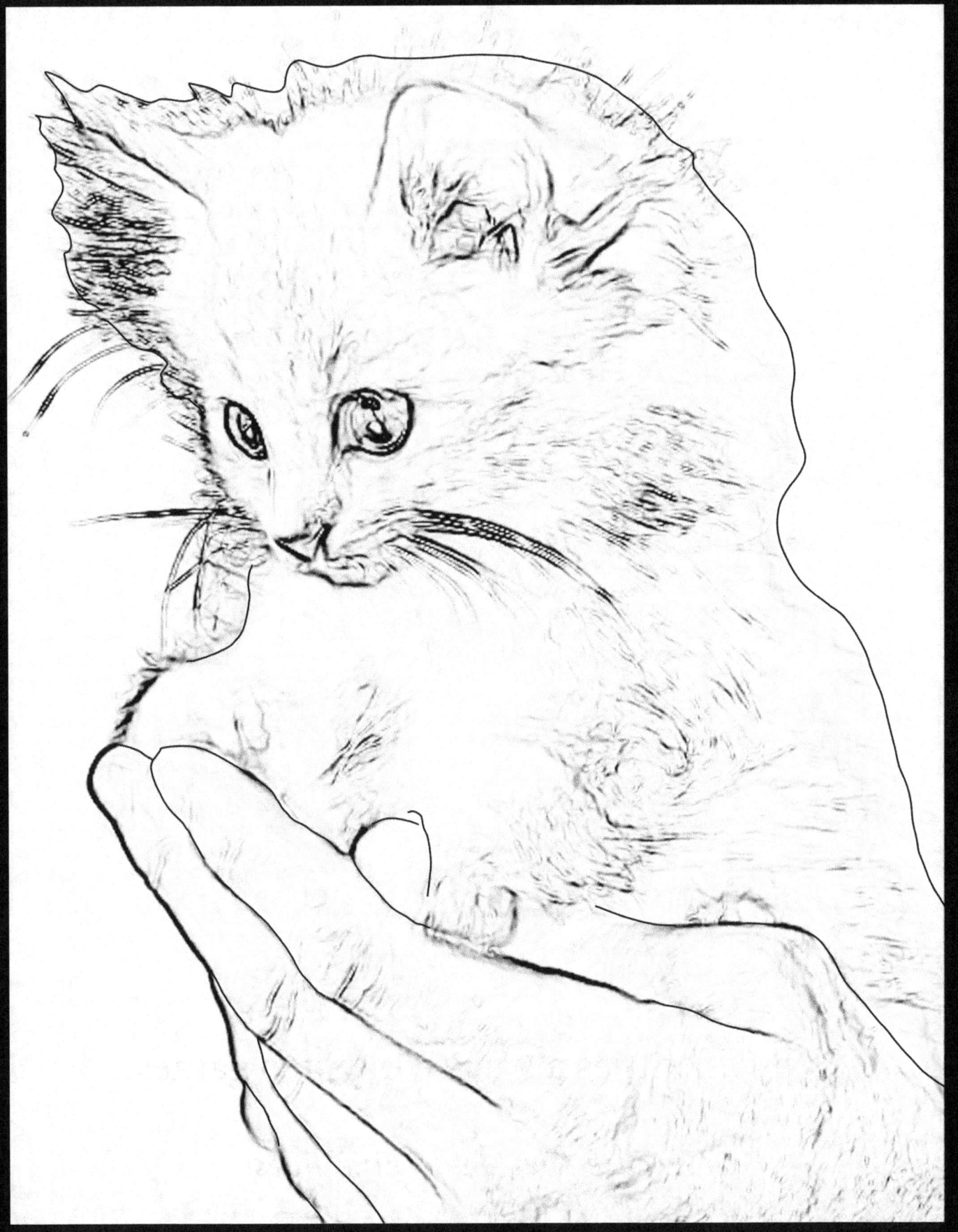

Why do kitties always win video games?

Because they have nine lives!

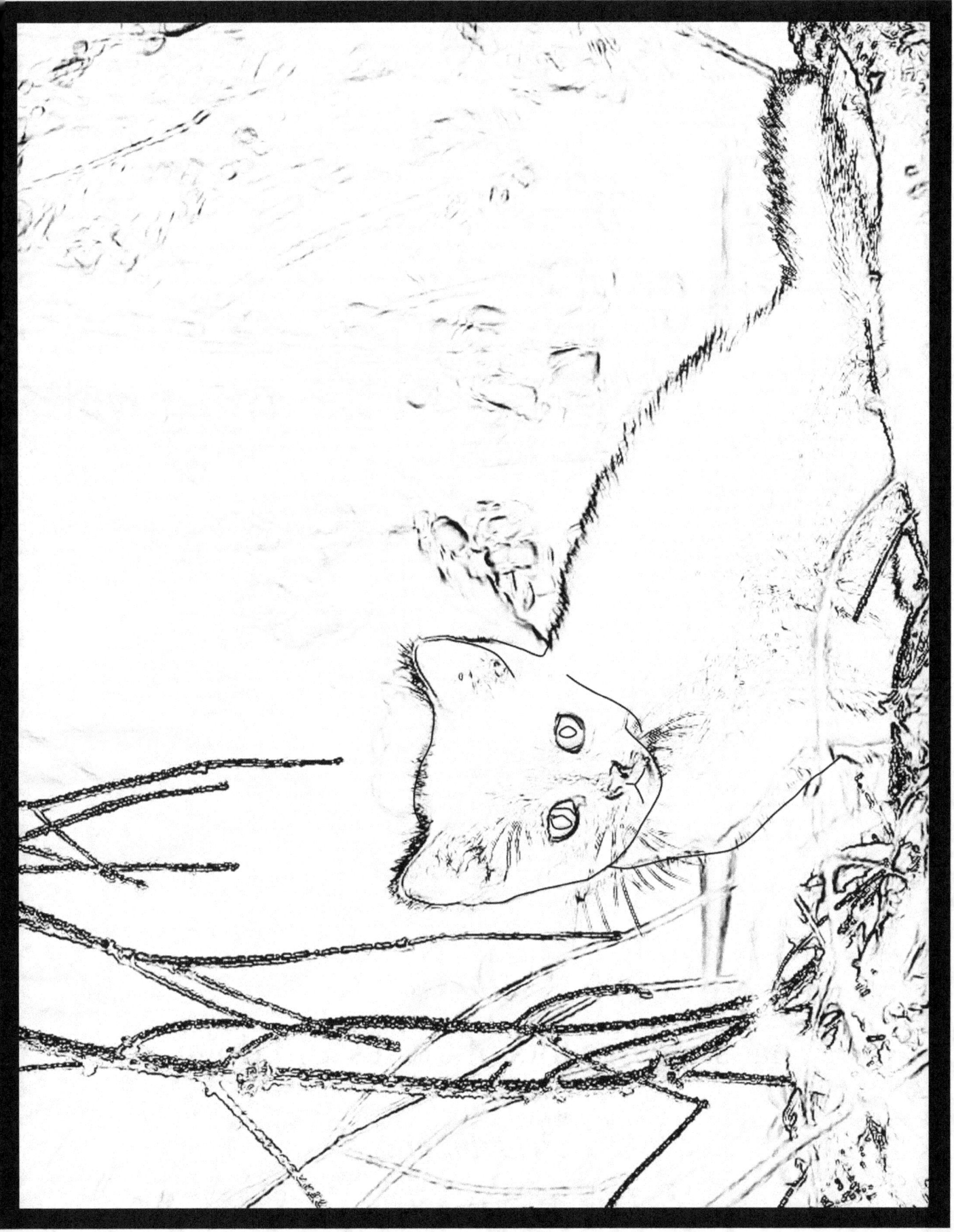

What state has lots of kitties and doggies?

Petsylvania!

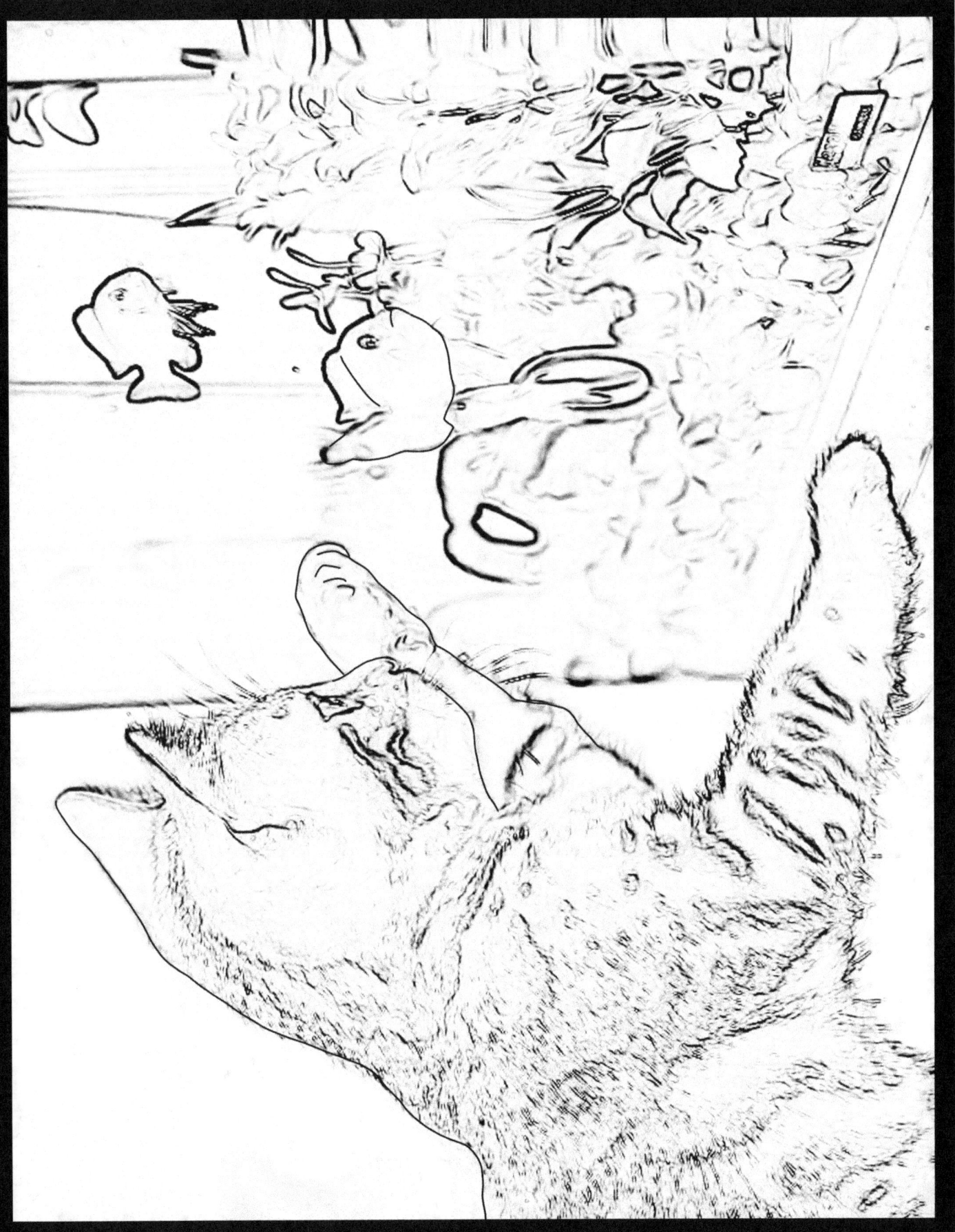

What do you call a pile of kitties?

A meowntain!

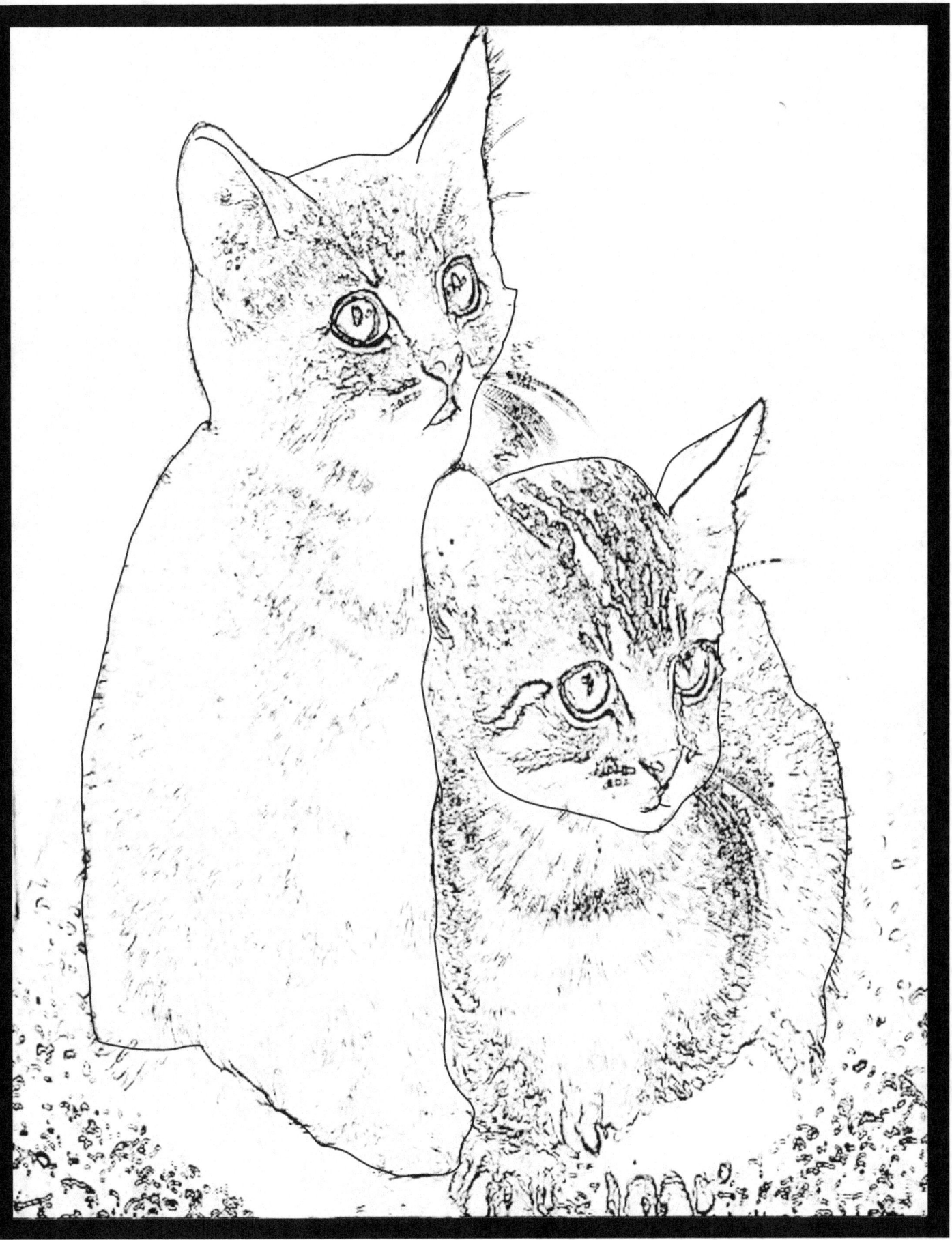

How does a kitty sing scales?

Doe-ray-mew!

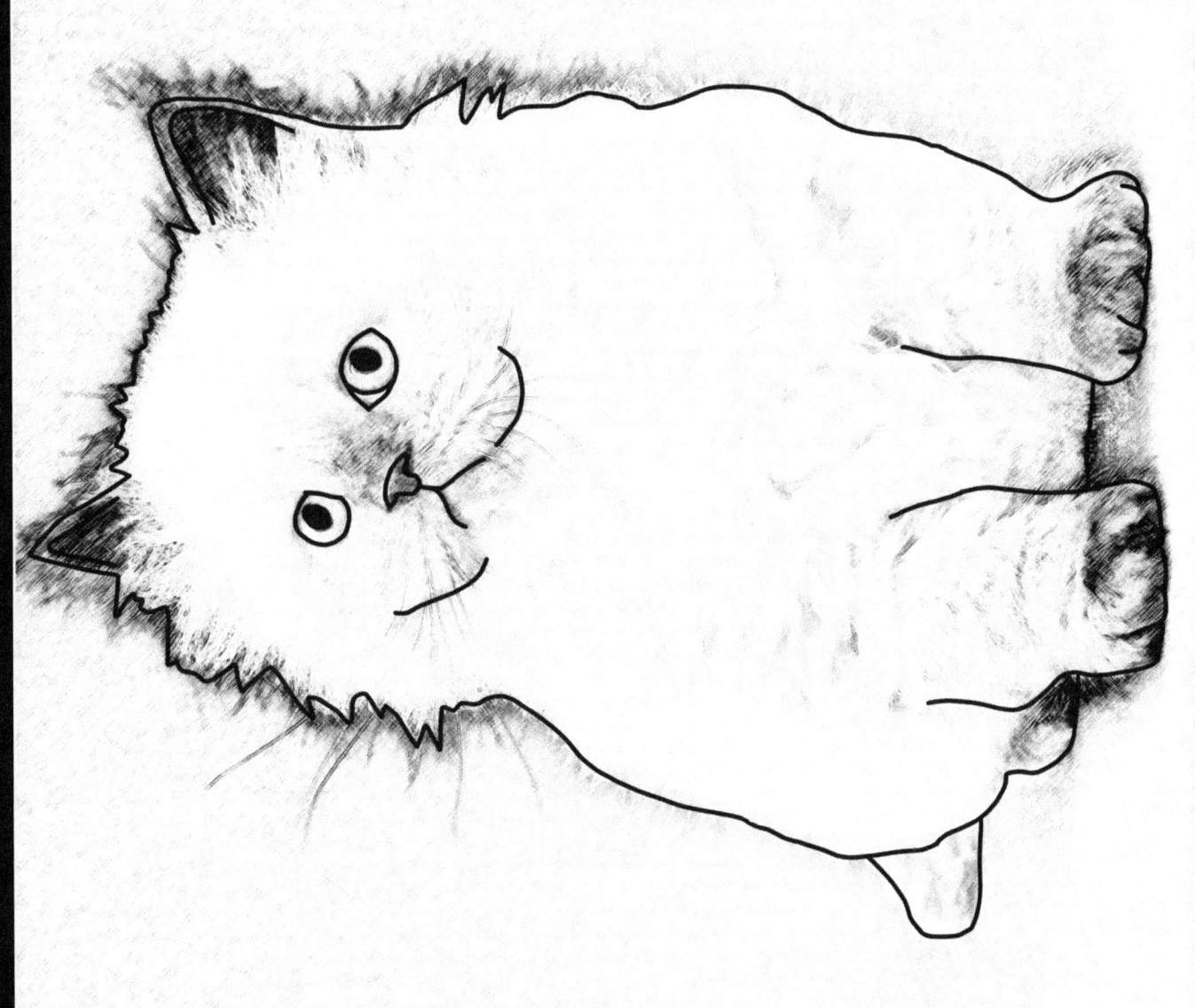

What do kitties eat for breakfast?

Mice Krispies!

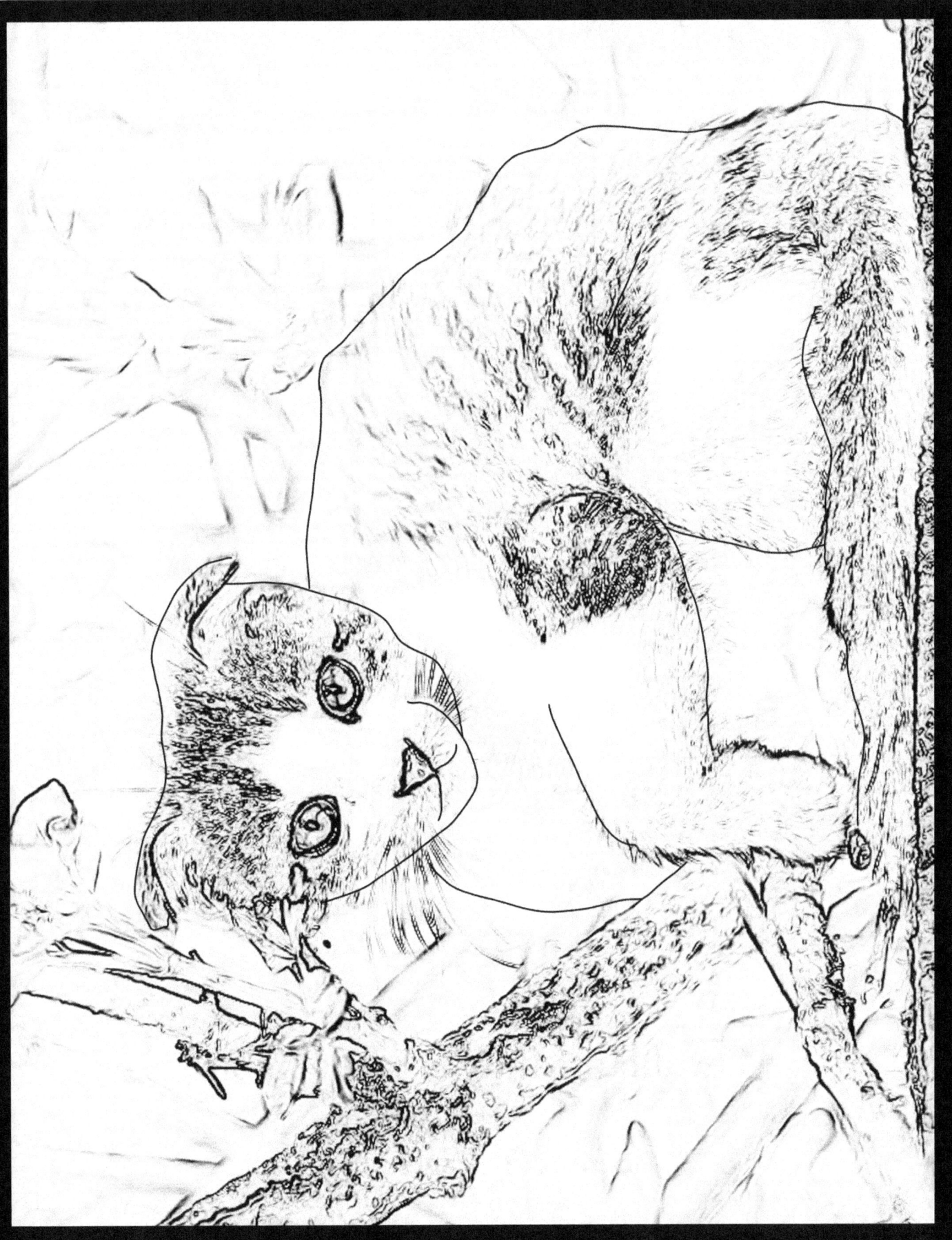

Why did the kitty eat the lemons?

She was a sourpuss!

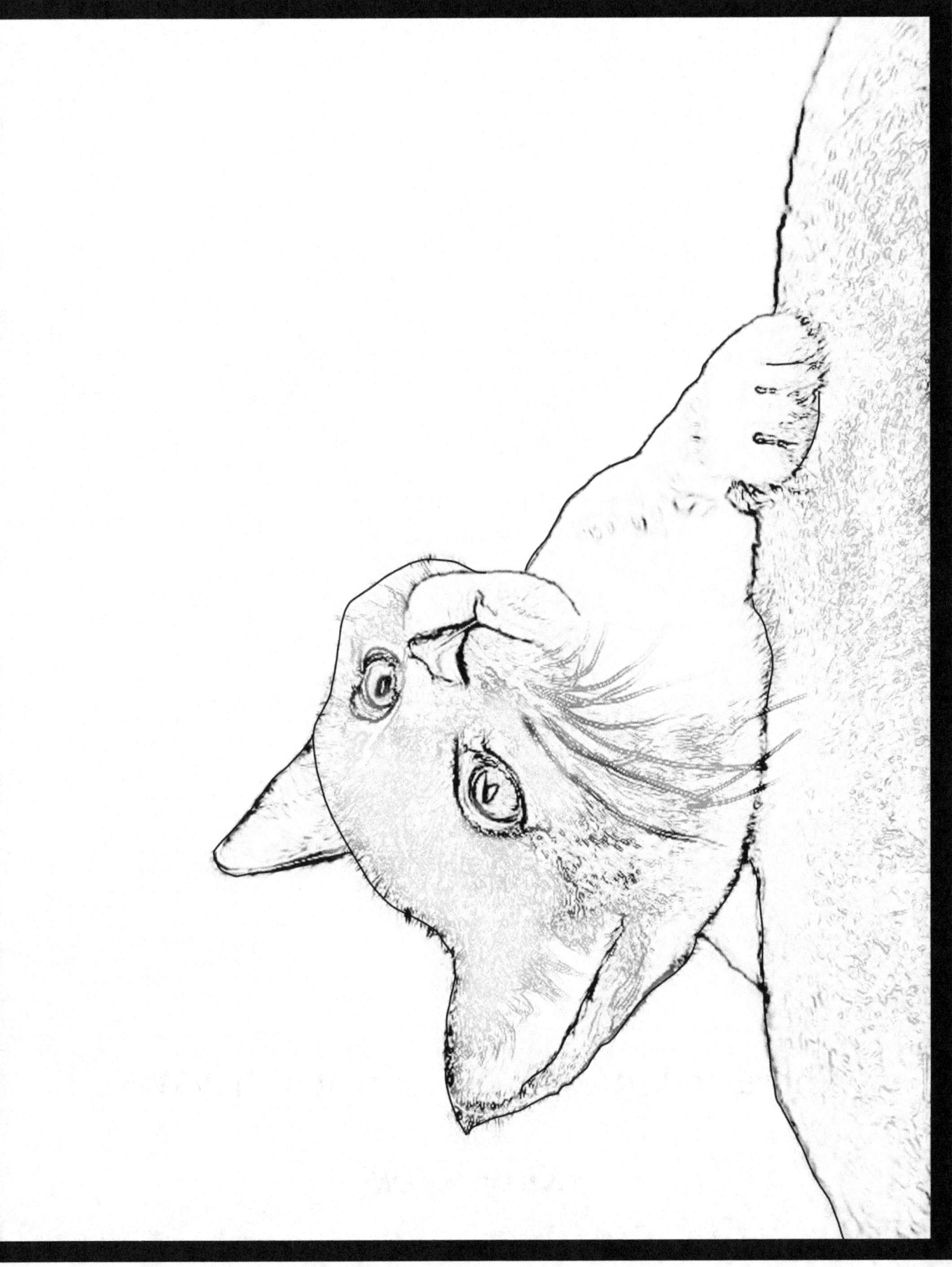

Where do kitties fly out of when they travel?

Kitty Hawk!

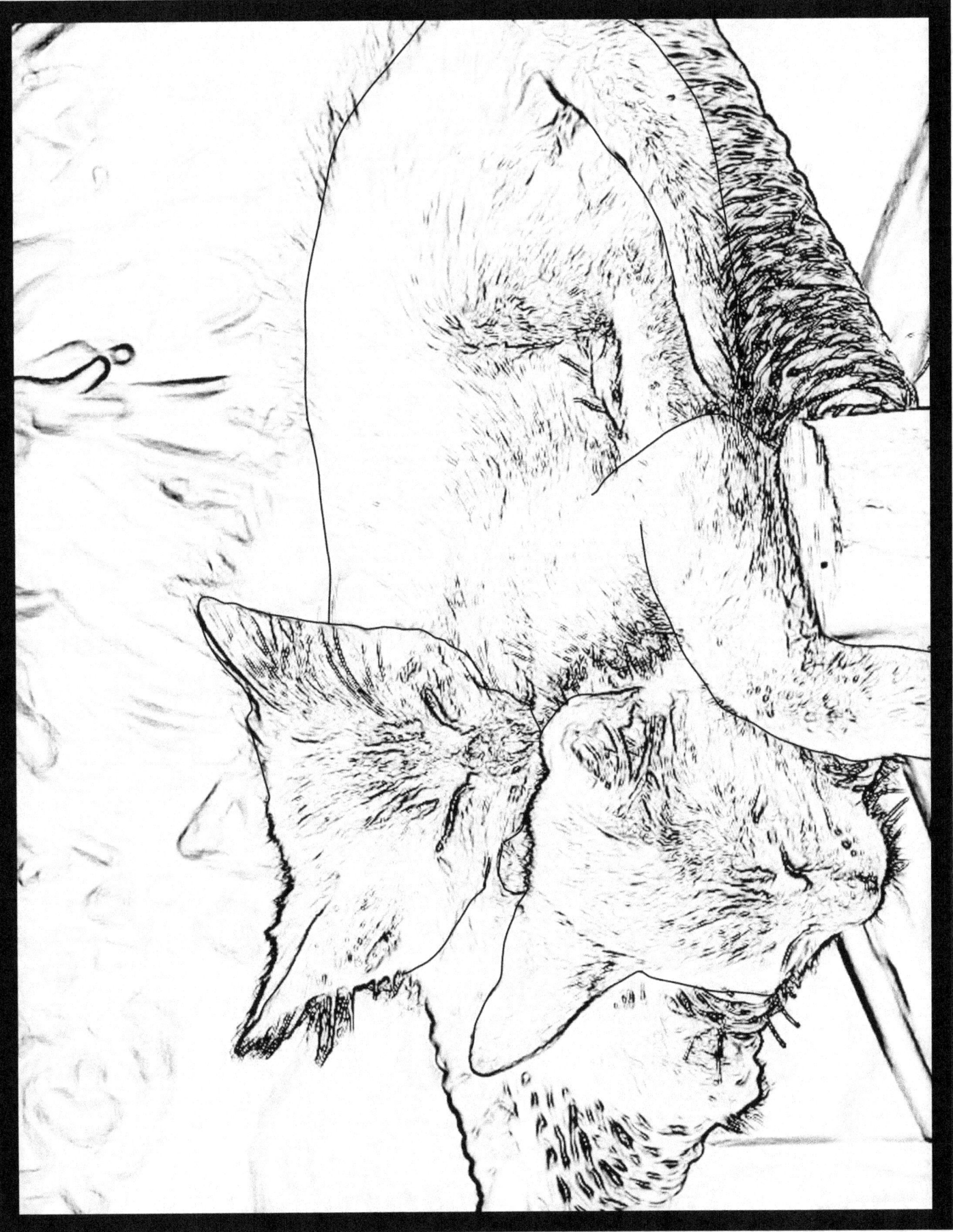

What's your kitty's favorite sport?

Hairball!

www.ingramcontent.com/pod-product-compliance
Lightning Source LLC
Chambersburg PA
CBHW080513220526
45465CB00006B/2472